knitted animal scarves,
mitts, and socks

knitted animal scarves, mitts, and socks

35 fun and fluffy creatures
to knit and wear

Fiona Goble

CICO BOOKS
LONDON NEW YORK

Published in 2015 by CICO Books
An imprint of Ryland Peters & Small Ltd
20–21 Jockey's Fields   341 E 116th St
London WC1R 4BW   New York, NY 10029

www.rylandpeters.com

10 9 8 7 6 5 4 3 2 1

Text © Fiona Goble 2015
Design and photography © CICO Books 2015

A CIP catalog record for this book is available
from the Library of Congress and the British
Library.

ISBN: 978-1-78249-252-8

Printed in China

Editor: Kate Haxell
Designer: Vicky Rankin
Photographer: Terry Benson
Stylist: Rob Merrett

In-house designer: Fahema Khanam
Art director: Sally Powell
Production controller: Mai-Ling Collyer
Publishing manager and editor: Penny Craig
Publisher: Cindy Richards

contents

introduction

Hot on the heels of the worldwide craze for knitted animal hats comes… knitted animal scarves. And for good measure, we've thrown in a few pairs of jaunty animal mitts and socks to keep your hands and feet feeling toasty, as well as your neck. So sit back, get out your yarn and needles, and rustle up a knitted fox stole and matching mitts—or any one of the 35 fun projects in this book.

On the following pages you'll find instructions to create countryside animal knits, such as the hedgehog mitts (page 19) and owl scarf (page 22). There are also some jungle animals including a monkey scarf (page 90) and tiger cowl (page 98). And who could forget the family pet knits, such as the cat scarves (pages 44 and 57), rabbit scarf (page 41), and dog scarf (page 51)? However, if you fancy something to remind you of days by the sea, you might want to try your hand at the penguin socks (page 80) or fish scarf (page 78)—or perhaps even our friendly wooly shark (page 70).

For a knit a little less ordinary, take a peek at the flamingo scarf (page 88), the honeycomb cowl complete with tiny bees (page 34) and—my personal favorite—the lovely green alligator scarf (page 72).

Some of the projects are for smaller children, but there are plenty of styles for older children—and for adults, you can easily add a few rows to most of the scarves to make them longer (just remember you may need to buy more yarn).

Most of the scarves are quite straightforward to knit and some are suitable for almost complete beginners. I've ranked the projects according to the level of skills required, from one to three symbols. Those with one symbol should be well within the scope of "advanced beginner" knitters, but it's a good idea to check through the instructions before buying your yarn, to make absolutely sure you feel confident.

The mitts and socks in the book are aimed at more experienced knitters, but if you've already knitted one-color gloves and socks and feel ready to work on something a little more exciting, they could be the perfect project to showcase your skills.

I've given details of all the yarns I've used in the book. You don't have to follow my choice exactly, but if you're knitting in a different yarn, make sure that you buy enough balls—the yardage for each ball is given for each pattern. And don't forget to knit a gauge square before you begin so that your project will be the right size.

I really hope you have fun knitting these projects—and don't forget, you don't have to stick to the colors we've chosen. Why not break out and create something unique—anyone for a crimson alligator?

Fiona Goble

country creatures

If farmyards and countryside rambles are high on your list of favorite things, check out the chirpy knits in this chapter. Choose from a softly sweet yellow duckling scarf or a wise owl mega-scarf. Or for the very little ones, how about a pair of super-cute mouse socks or a honeycomb cowl with bees?

duckling scarf

Who can resist a tiny, fluffy yellow duck? Well, not me. This wonderfully cute scarf is knitted in a combination of wool and mohair to make sure that it's not just soft and fuzzy, but is also super warm. I think it would look great with a bright yellow PVC mac and sou'wester—or just about anything, come to think of it.

Yarn
Rowan Kid Classic (70% wool, 26% mohair, 4% nylon) worsted (Aran) yarn
1 x 1¾oz (50g) ball (153yd/140m) in shade 870 Rosewood (A)
Patons Merino Extrafine DK (100% wool) light worsted (DK) yarn
1 x 1¾oz (50g) ball (131yd/120m) in shade 00120 Sundance (B)
Rowan Kidsilk Haze (70% mohair, 30% silk) lace weight yarn
1 x ¾oz (25g) ball (230yd/210m) in shade 663 Essence (C)
Small amounts of black and off-white light worsted (DK) yarns

Needles and equipment
US 9 (5.5mm) knitting needles
Yarn sewing needle
Large-eyed embroidery needle

Gauge (tension)
17 sts and 20 rows in stockinette (stocking) stitch to a 4-in (10-cm) square on US 9 (5.5mm) needles using B and C held together.

Measurements
The finished scarf is 41¼in (105cm) long.

Abbreviations
See page 126.

To make scarf
Cast on 2 sts in A.
Row 1: [Inc] twice. *(4 sts)*
Row 2: K1, p2, k1.
Row 3: K1, m1, k to last st, m1, k1. *(6 sts)*
Row 4: K1, p to last st, k1.
Rep last 2 rows 6 times more. *(18 sts)*
Break A and join in B and C, using the two yarns held together.
Row 17: K2, m1, k to last 2 sts, m1, k2. *(20 sts)*
Row 18: K2, p to last 2 sts, k2.
Rep last 2 rows twice more. *(24 sts)*
Row 23: Knit.
Row 24: K2, p to last 2 sts, k2.
Rep rows 23–24, 81 times more.
Shape tail
Row 187: K7, turn. Work on 7 sts just knitted only, leaving rem sts on needle.

Next row: Ssk, p to last 2 sts, k2tog. *(7 sts)*
Rep last 2 rows once more. *(3 sts)*
Next row: K3tog. *(1 st)*
Break yarn and fasten off.**
Rejoin yarn to rem sts on RS of work.
Next row: [K1, k2tog] 3 times, k1, turn. Work on 7 sts just knitted only, leaving rem sts on needle.
Next row: K2, p to last 2 sts, k2.
Next row: K3, [k1, p1, k1 all into next st], k3.
Next row: K2, p to last 2 sts, k2.
Rep from * to ** once more.
Rejoin yarn to rem sts on RS of work.
Next row: Knit.
Rep from * to ** once more.

To make up
Using black yarn, embroider two coils of chain stitch (see page 124) for the centers of the eyes. Work a ring of chain stitch around each eye center using off-white yarn. Using black yarn, work two straight stitches (see page 124) on the beak for the nostrils.
Weave in all loose ends.

***Next row:** K2, p to last 2 sts, k2.
Next row: K3, [k1, p1, k1 all into next st], k3. *(9 sts)*
Next row: K2, p to last 2 sts, k2.
Next row: Ssk, k2, [k1, p1, k1 all into next st], k2, k2tog.
Next row: K2, p to last 2 sts, k2.
Rep last 2 rows, 5 times more.
Next row: K4, [k1, p1, k1 all into next st], k4. *(11 sts)*
Next row: K2, p to last 2 sts, k2.
Next row: K5, [k1, p1, k1 all into next st], k5. *(13 sts)*
Next row: Ssk, p to last 2 sts, k2tog. *(11 sts)*
Next row: Ssk, k to last 2 sts, k2tog. *(9 sts)*

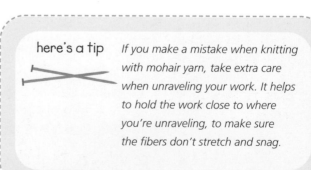

here's a tip *If you make a mistake when knitting with mohair yarn, take extra care when unraveling your work. It helps to hold the work close to where you're unraveling, to make sure the fibers don't stretch and snag.*

owl socks

If you haven't yet got your fair share of all things owl, here is your chance to stand out from the crowd and knit a pair of owl socks. The socks can be knitted on a set of double-pointed needles or a short circular needle. Both take a bit of getting used to if you haven't worked in this way before, but the pattern itself is very simple. I've knitted these owls in shades of rust and ochre, but you can knit yours in any color you like: keep it realistic or take a flight of fancy.

Yarn and materials

Rowan Pure Wool DK (100% wool) light worsted (DK) yarn
1 x 1¾oz (50g) ball (142yd/130m) in shade 049
Ox Blood (A)
1 x 1¾oz (50g) ball (142yd/130m) in shade 051 Gold (B)
Small amount of light worsted (DK) yarn in off-white (C)
Small amount of light worsted (DK) yarn in turquoise (D)
Small amount of light worsted (DK) yarn in gray (E)
4 x ⅜-in (10-mm) black buttons

Needles and equipment

US 8 (5mm) knitting needles
A set of 4 (or 5) US 6 (4mm) double-pointed needles
(DPNs) or a US 6 (4mm) short circular needle designed for
knitting socks and other smaller items (see page 122 for
more information on knitting on DPNs and circular needles)
US 2/3 (3mm) knitting needles
Stitch marker or small safety pin
Yarn sewing needle

Gauge (tension)

22 sts and 30 rows in stockinette (stocking) stich to a 4-in
(10-cm) square on US 6 (4mm) needles.

Measurements

The finished socks measure 6¾in (17cm) from the heel
to the tip of the toe. They should fit a child's shoe size
US 11½–12½ (UK 10½–11½/EU 29–30).

Abbreviations

See page 126.

To make socks

Make 2

Using US 8 (5mm) needles, cast on 40 sts in A. Transfer sts to
DPNs or circular needle and mark your first cast-on stitch
with stitch marker or small safety pin.
Round 1: [K2, p2] to end.
Rep round 1, 4 times more.
Break A and join in B.
Knit 30 rounds.
Shape heel back
Break B and join in A.
Row 1: K10, turn. *(10 sts)*
Row 2: P20. *(20 sts)*
(If using DPNs, keep all 20 sts on one needle.)
Row 3: [Sl1, k1] to end.
Row 4: Sl1 pwise, p to end.

Rep rows 3–4, 9 times more.

Shape heel base

Row 23: K12, ssk, k1, turn. *(19 sts)*

Row 24: Sl1 pwise, p5, p2tog, p1, turn. *(18 sts)*

Row 25: Sl1, k6, ssk, k1, turn. *(17 sts)*

Row 26: Sl1 pwise, p7, p2tog, p1, turn. *(16 sts)*

Row 27: Sl1, k8, ssk, k1, turn. *(15 sts)*

Row 28: Sl1 pwise, p9, p2tog, p1, turn. *(14 sts)*

Row 29: Sl1, k10, ssk, turn. *(13 sts)*

Row 30: Sl1, p10, p2tog, turn. *(12 sts)*

Shape foot

Break A and join in B. Work remainder of sock in B.

Row 31 and forming base for rounds: Knit, putting stitch marker or safety pin between 6th and 7th sts to mark back of sock. With empty needle if using DPNs, pick up and k 10 sts up first side of heel back then k across 20 sts of top part of sock.

With another empty needle if using DPNs, pick up and k 10 sts down side of second heel back and then k 6 sts along base of heel (to stitch marker). These 52 sts will form the foot part of the sock.

Round 1: K13, k2tog, k22, ssk, k13. *(50 sts)*

Round 2: Knit.

Round 3: K12, k2tog, k22, ssk, k12. *(48 sts)*

Round 4: Knit.

Round 5: K11, k2tog, k22, ssk, k11. *(46 sts)*

Round 6: Knit.

Round 7: K10, k2tog, k22, ssk, k10. *(44 sts)*

Round 8: Knit.

Round 9: K9, k2tog, k22, ssk, k9. *(42 sts)*

Round 10: Knit.

Round 11: K8, k2tog, k22, ssk, k8. *(40 sts)*

Knit 23 more rounds.

Shape toe

Round 1: K7, ssk, k2, k2tog, k14, ssk, k2, k2tog, k7. *(36 sts)*

Round 2: Knit.

Round 1: K6, ssk, k2, k2tog, k12, ssk, k2, k2tog, k6. *(32 sts)*

Round 2: Knit.

Round 3: K5, ssk, k2, k2tog, k10, ssk, k2, k2tog, k5. *(28 sts)*

Round 4: Knit.

Round 5: K4, ssk, k2, k2tog, k8, ssk, k2, k2tog, k4. *(24 sts)*

Round 6: Knit.

Round 7: K3, ssk, k2, k2tog, k6, ssk, k2, k2tog, k3. *(20 sts)*

Round 8: K2, ssk, k2, k2tog, k4, ssk, k2, k2tog, k2. *(16 sts)*

Round 9: K1, ssk, k2, k2tog, k2, ssk, k2, k2tog, k1. *(12 sts)*

Break yarn, thread it through rem sts, and pull up securely.

Eye bases

Make 4

Using US 2/3 (3mm) needles, cast on 24 sts in C.

Row 1: Knit.

Row 2: [P2tog] to end. *(12 sts)*

Row 3: Knit.

Row 4: [P2tog] to end. *(6 sts)*

Break yarn, thread it through rem sts, and pull up securely.

Eye fringes

Make 4

Using US 2/3 (3mm) needles, cast on 3 sts in D.

*Bind (cast) off 2 sts, transfer rem st from right to left needle without turning work. One picot made.

Cast on 2 sts.**

Rep from * to ** till you have 12 picots. Fasten off.

Beak

Make 2

Using US 2/3 (3mm) needles, cast on 4 sts in E.

Beg with a k row, work 2 rows in st st.

Row 3: Ssk, k2tog. *(2 sts)*

Row 4: P2tog. *(1 st)*

Break yarn and fasten off.

To make up

For the eyes, fold the eye bases in half so that the RS is on the inside and oversew (see page 125) the seam (row edges) to form a disc. Oversew the eye bases in place on the front ankle part of the socks, near the top. Oversew the picot edging in place around eye bases. Sew the buttons in place in the centers of the eyes.

Oversew the beaks in place.

Weave in all loose ends.

here's a tip

If you want to make your socks quicker and simpler to complete, you can use big buttons sewn on with white yarn for the eyes, instead of knitting the eye pieces.

lamb scarf

There's something super-cute about creating a lamb out of lambswool—so there's no way I was going to miss this one out of the collection. The scarf is knitted in a soft wool-rich yarn that I've combined with a light-as-a-feather mohair yarn, to make it even fluffier. With its black feet and soulful eyes, this scarf will brighten the life of anyone who wears it.

Yarn

King Cole Magnum Lightweight Chunky (75% acrylic, 25% wool) bulky (chunky) yarn
1 x 3½oz (100g) ball (120yd/110m) in shade 010 Champagne (A)
1 x 3½oz (100g) ball (120yd/110m) in shade 187 Charcoal (D)
Phildar Nebuleuse (41% wool, 41% acrylic, 18% nylon) bulky (chunky) yarn
2 x 1¾oz (50g) balls (56yd/51m) in shade 0032 Ecru (B)
Wendy Air (70% kid mohair, 30% nylon) lace weight yarn
1 x ¾oz (25g) ball (218yd/200m) in shade 2612 Lottie (C)

Needles and equipment

US 10 (6mm) knitting needles
US 10½/11 (7mm) knitting needles
Yarn sewing needle
Large-eyed embroidery needle

Gauge (tension)

14 sts and 16 rows in stockinette (stocking) stitch to a 4-in (10-cm) square on US 10½/11 (7mm) needles using B and C held together.

Measurements

The finished scarf is 47¼in (120cm) long, including back legs.

Abbreviations

See page 126.

To make scarf

Using US 10 (6mm) needles, cast on 6 sts in A.
Row 1: Inc, k3, inc, k1. *(8 sts)*
Row 2: Purl.
Row 3: K1, m1, k to last st, m1, k1. *(10 sts)*
Row 4: Purl.
Rep rows 3–4, 5 times more. *(20 sts)*
Beg with a k row, work 8 rows in st st.
Row 23: K2tog, k to last 2 sts, k2tog. *(18 sts)*
Break A and join in B and C, using the two yarns held together.
Change to US 10½/11 (7mm) needles.
Row 24: Knit.
Row 25: K2, p to last 2 sts, k2.
Knit 2 rows.
Rep rows 24–27 (last 4 rows), 32 times more.
Row 156: Knit.
Row 157: Purl.
Bind (cast) off.

Face

Using US 10 (6mm) needles, cast on 6 sts in A.
Row 1: Inc, k3, inc, k1. *(8 sts)*
Row 2: Purl.
Row 3: K1, m1, k to last st, m1, k1. *(10 sts)*
Row 4: Purl.
Rep rows 3–4, 5 times more. *(20 sts)*
Beg with a k row, work 8 rows in st st.
Bind (cast) off.

Front leg

Make 2
Using US 10 (6mm) needles, cast on 6 sts in A.
Knit 16 rows.
Break A and join in D.
Beg with a k row, work 10 rows in st st.
Shape foot
Row 27: Ssk, k to last 2 sts, k2tog. *(4 sts)*
Row 28: Purl.

Tail

Using US 10½/11 (7mm) needles, cast on 6 sts with B and C held together.
Beg with a k row, work 8 rows in st st.
Row 9: Skpo, k2, k2tog. *(4 sts)*
Row 10: [P2tog] twice. *(2 sts)*
Row 11: K2tog. *(1 st)*
Break yarn and fasten off.

Fringe

Using US 10½/11 (7mm) needles, cast on 7 sts with B and C held together.
Row 1: Knit—winding your yarn around the needle 4 times for each st.
Row 2: Knit, dropping extra loops on each stitch.
Bind (cast) off.

To make up

On face, using a separated strand of D, embroider two circles for the eyes and the lines for the nose in chain stitch (see page 124). Using a single strand of D, work three straight stitches (see page 124) above each eye for the lashes.
Place the face on the head part of the main scarf so that the right sides are together. Oversew (see page 125) the side seams. Turn the head the right way out and sew the top edge in place using mattress stitch (see page 125).
Oversew the front legs in place underneath the head, where the head meets the main part of the scarf.
Fold the ear pieces in half so that the right sides are on the inside. Oversew around the sides leaving the lower (cast-on) edge open for turning. Turn and oversew the lower edge. Oversew the ears in place using the photograph as a guide.
Fold the fringe in half lengthwise to form a row of loops. Oversew in place.
Sew the back seam of the tail using flat stitch (see page 125). Oversew the tail in place in the center of the lamb's lower end, just where the garter stitch border meets the main part of the scarf.
Sew back legs to bound- (cast-) off edge of scarf.
Weave in all loose ends.

Row 29: Ssk, k2tog. *(2 sts)*
Row 30: Skpo. *(1 st)*
Break yarn and fasten off.

Back leg

Make 2
Using US 10 (6mm) needles, cast on 6 sts in A.
Knit 12 rows.
Break A and join in D.
Beg with a k row, work 10 rows in st st.
Shape foot
Row 23: Ssk, k to last 2 sts, k2tog. *(4 sts)*
Row 24: Purl.
Row 25: Ssk, k2tog. *(2 sts)*
Row 26: Skpo. *(1 st)*
Break yarn and fasten off.

Ear

Make 2
Using US 10 (6mm) needles, cast on 5 sts in A.
Beg with a k row, work 5 rows in st st.
Row 6: P2tog, p1, p2tog. *(3 sts)*
Row 7: [Inc] twice, k1. *(5 sts)*
Beg with a p row, work 5 rows in st st.
Bind (cast) off.

hedgehog mitts

Who can resist a cute little hedgehog—especially ones that are prickle-free with not a flea in sight—making these the perfect mittens to keep small hands warm in winter. I've knitted the back of these mitts in a gorgeous milky brown, 100% wool yarn, and teamed it with a super-soft beige yarn for the little animal's snout. The textured knit on the back of the mittens is very simple to work, but gives a lovely rough feel to the knitting to suggest the hedgehog's spines.

Yarn
Erika Knight Vintage Wool (100% wool) worsted (Aran) yarn
1 x 1¾oz (50g) ball (95yd/87m) in shade 044 Milk Chocolate (A)
Debbie Bliss Cashmerino Aran (55% wool, 33% acrylic, 12% cashmere) worsted (Aran) yarn
1 x 1¾oz (50g) ball (98yd/90m) in shade 102 Beige (B)
Small amount of black light worsted (DK) yarn

Needles and equipment
US 8 (5mm) knitting needles
Yarn sewing needle
Large-eyed embroidery needle

Gauge (tension)
18 sts and 24 rows in stockinette (stocking) stitch to a 4-in (10-cm) square on US 8 (5mm) needles (for both yarns).

Measurements
The finished mittens measure 7½in (19cm) from the base of the wrist to the tip and should fit an average size child of 7–10 years.

Abbreviations
See page 126.

Left mitten
Cast on 34 sts in A.
Row 1: [K2, p2] to last 2 sts, k2.
Row 2: [P2, k2] to last 2 sts, p2.
Rep rows 1–2, 3 times more.
Row 9: K17, [p1, k1] to last st, p1.
Row 10: [K1, p1] 9 times, p to end.
Row 11: K18, [p1, k1] to end.
Row 12: [P1, k1] 8 times, p to end.
Row 13: K14, inc, k1, inc, [p1, k1] to last st, p1. *(36 sts)*
Row 14: [K1, p1] 8 times, k1, p to end.
Row 15: K14, inc, k3, inc, k1, [p1, k1] to end. *(38 sts)*
Row 16: [P1, k1] 8 times, p to end.
Row 17: K14, inc, k5, inc, [p1, k1] to last st, p1. *(40 sts)*
Row 18: [K1, p1] 8 times, k1, p to end.

Row 45: K1, skpo, k1, k2tog, k2, skpo, k1, k2tog, k1. *(10 sts)*
Break yarn, thread it through rem sts, and pull up securely.

Right mitten

Cast on 34 sts in A.
Rows 1–8: Work as for left mitten.
Row 9: [P1, k1] 8 times, p1, k to end.
Row 10: P17, [k1, p1] to last st, k1.
Row 11: [K1, p1] 8 times, k to end.
Row 12: P18, [k1, p1] to end.
Row 13: [P1, k1] 8 times, p1, inc, k1, inc, k to end. *(36 sts)*
Row 14: P19, [k1, p1] to last st, k1.
Row 15: [K1, p1] 8 times, k1, inc, k3, inc, k to end. *(38 sts)*
Row 16: P22, [k1, p1] to end.
Row 17: [P1, k1] 8 times, p1, inc, k5, inc, k to end. *(40 sts)*
Row 18: P23, [k1, p1] to last st, k1.
Row 19: [K1, p1] 8 times, k1, inc, k7, inc, k to end. *(42 sts)*
Row 20: P26, [k1, p1] to end.
Row 21: [P1, k1] 8 times, p1, k to end.
Row 22: P25, [k1, p1] to last st, k1.

Shape thumb

Next row: [K1, p1] 8 times, k11, turn and cast on 1 st.
Work remainder of thumb as for right mitten, beg at *.
With RS facing, rejoin yarn and pick up and k 2 sts across base of thumb then k to end. *(34 sts)*
Row 24: P16, [k1, p1] to end.
Row 25: [P1, k1] 9 times, k to end.
Row 26: P17, [k1, p1] to end.
Row 27: [K1, p1] 9 times, k to end.
Rep rows 24–27 twice more.
Row 36: P16, [k1, p1] to end.
Break A, join in B, and work remainder of mitten in B.
Row 37: Work as for left mitten to complete.

To make up

Join the side seams of the mittens using flat stitch (see page 125).
Using black yarn, embroider a small circle of chain stitch (see page 124) for the eyes and a larger circle of chain stitch for the nose.
Weave in all loose ends.

Row 19: K14, inc, k7, inc, [k1, p1] to last st, k1. *(42 sts)*
Row 20: [P1, k1] 8 times, p to end.
Row 21: K25, [p1, k1] to last st, p1.
Row 22: [K1, p1] 8 times, k1, p to end.

Shape thumb

Next row: K24, turn and cast on 1 st.
***Next row:** P11, turn and cast on 1 st.
Work on these 12 sts just worked, leaving rem sts on needles.
Beg with a k row, work 6 rows in st st.
Next row: K1, [k2tog, k2] twice, k2tog, k1. *(9 sts)*
Next row: Purl.
Next row: [K1, k2tog] 3 times. *(6 sts)*
Break yarn, thread it through rem sts, and pull up securely.
With RS facing, rejoin yarn and pick up and k 2 sts across base of thumb then [p1, k1] to end. *(34 sts)*
Row 24: [P1, k1] 9 times, p to end.
Row 25: K15, [p1, k1] to last st, p1.
Row 26: [K1, p1] 9 times, k1, p to end.
Row 27: K16, [p1, k1] to end.
Rep rows 24–27 twice more.
Row 36: [P1, k1] 9 times, p to end.
Break A, join in B, and work remainder of mitten in B.
Row 37: K2, [skpo, k2] 4 times, [k2tog, k2] to end. *(26 sts)*
Beg with a p row, work 3 rows in st st.
Row 41: K2, [skpo] twice, k1, [k2tog] twice, k4, [skpo] twice, k1, [k2tog] twice, k2. *(18 sts)*
Row 42: Purl.
Row 43: K2, skpo, k1, k2tog, k4, skpo, k1, k2tog, k2. *(14 sts)*
Row 44: Purl.

owl scarf

If a woodland walk is what you fancy, why not dress the part and kit yourself out in this super owl scarf with pockets at the ends to keep your hands extra toasty. The scarf is knitted in a tweedy yarn, and in a super-chunky weight that means your knitting grows almost magically fast. I've added the accents and trim in autumnal shades of ochre and rust—but shades like pink and purple would work brilliantly as well.

Yarn
Lion Brand Wool-Ease Thick & Quick (82% acrylic, 10% wool, 8% rayon) super-bulky (super-chunky) yarn
2 x 6oz (170g) balls (106yd/97m) in shade 123 Oatmeal (A)
Katia Maxi Merino Chunky (55% wool, 45% acrylic) bulky (chunky) yarn
1 x 3½oz (100g) ball (137yd/125m) in shade 047 Gold (B)
1 x 3½oz (100g) ball (137yd/125m) in shade 040 Rust (C)
Small amount of dark brown light worsted (DK) yarn

Needles and equipment
US 13 (9mm) knitting needles
US 9 (5.5mm) knitting needles
N-13 (9mm) crochet hook (or a similar size hook)
J-10 (6mm) crochet hook (or a similar size hook)
Yarn sewing needle
Large-eyed embroidery needle
4 x ¾in (18mm) cream buttons

Gauge (tension)
9 sts and 12 rows in stockinette (stocking) stitch to a 4-in (10-cm) square on US 13 (9mm) needles.

Measurements
The finished scarf is 58½in (149cm) long.

Abbreviations
See page 126.

To make scarf
Using US 13 (9mm) needles, cast on 13 sts in A.
Row 1: Knit.
Row 2: Knit.
Beg with a k row, work 17 rows in st st.
Row 20: Knit.
Row 21: Purl.
Rep rows 20–21, 87 times more.
Row 196: Knit.
Beg with a k row, work 17 rows in st st.
Row 214: Knit.
Bind (cast) off.

Eye bases
Make 4
Using US 9 (5.5mm) needles, cast on 24 sts in B.
Row 1: Knit.

Cast on 2 sts.**
Rep from * to ** till you have 12 picots. Fasten off.

Ear loops
Using the J-10 (6mm) crochet hook and a doubled strand of dark brown yarn, work 4 x 5-in (13-cm) crochet chains.

To make up
Fold the pocket tops at each end of the scarf upward so that the right side of the top part of the pocket is on the inside and oversew (see page 125) the side seams. Turn the pockets the right way out.
Using B doubled and the N-13 (9mm) crochet hook, work a crochet edging (see page 123) along the sides of the scarf, beginning and ending at the top of the pockets.
For the eyes, fold the eye base pieces in half so that the right side is on the inside and oversew the seam (row edges) to form a disc. Oversew the eye bases in position. Oversew the picot edging in place around eye bases and sew the buttons in place in the centers of the eyes using the dark brown yarn. Using dark brown yarn, work a teardrop-shape for the beak in chain stitch (see page 124). Make each dark brown crochet chain into two loops and stitch in place at the top corners of the pockets for the ears.
Weave in all loose ends.

Row 2: [P2tog] to end. *(12 sts)*
Row 3: [K2tog] to end. *(6 sts)*
Break yarn, thread it through rem sts, and pull up securely.

Eye fringes
Make 4
Using US 9 (5.5mm) needles, cast on 3 sts in C.
*Bind (cast) off 2 sts, transfer rem st from right to left needle without turning work. One picot made.

mouse scarf

You may not want a real-life rodent anywhere near your neck—and I don't blame you a bit—but I'm sure you'll like the feel of this mouse scarf, knitted in a lovely soft yarn with a touch of silk and cashmere, and in the softest shade of pale gray. The scarf is shorter than most of the others in this book, so would make a great choice for a smaller child—though I know big kids will love it too.

Yarn
Sublime Baby Cashmere Merino Silk DK (75% wool, 20% silk, 5% cashmere) light worsted (DK) yarn
1 x 1¾oz (50g) ball (126yd/116m) in shade 001 Piglet (A)
Rowan Pure Wool DK (100% wool) light worsted (DK) yarn
1 x 1¾oz (50g) ball (142yd/130m) in shade 00002 Shale (B)
Small amounts of black and beige light worsted (DK) yarn

Needles and equipment
US 6 (4mm) knitting needles
Yarn sewing needle
Large-eyed embroidery needle

Gauge (tension)
22 sts and 30 rows in stockinette (stocking) stitch to a 4-in (10-cm) square on US 6 (4mm) needles using B.

Measurements
The finished scarf is 33in (84cm) long, including the back legs.

Abbreviations
See page 126.

To make scarf
Cast on 4 sts in A.
Row 1: [Inc, k1] twice. *(6 sts)*
Row 2: Purl.
Row 3: K1, m1, k to last st, m1, k1. *(8 sts)*
Row 4: Purl.
Break A and join in B.
Row 5: K1, m1, k to last st, m1, k1. *(10 sts)*
Row 6: Purl.
Rep rows 5–6, 7 times more. *(24 sts)*
Beg with a k row, work 12 rows in st st.
Row 33: Knit.
Row 34: Knit.
Row 35: K2, p to last 2 sts, k2.
Rep rows 34–35, 97 times more.
Knit 3 rows.
Shape back legs
Row 233: K6, bind (cast) off 12 sts, k to end.
Work on last 6 sts only, leaving rem 6 sts on needle.
Knit 4 rows.

Break B and join in A.

Beg with a k row, work 14 rows in st st.

Shape paw

*Next row: K2, turn and work on these 2 sts only, leaving rem sts on needle.

**Beg with a p row, work 3 rows in st st.

Next row: Skpo, [pick up and k 1 st from row ends, bind (cast) off st] twice down side of toe.*** (1 st)

Next row: K1 st from left needle, bind (cast) off 1 st, k1. (2 sts)

Rep from ** to *** once more.

Beg with a p row, work 3 rows in st st.

Next row: Skpo, [pick up and k 1 st from row ends, bind (cast) off st] twice down side of toe. (1 st)

Fasten off.*

Rejoin B to rem sts on RS of work.

Knit 4 rows.

Break B and join in A.

Beg with a k row, work 14 rows st st.

Shape paw

Rep from * to *.

Face

Cast on 4 sts in A.

Row 1: [Inc, k1] twice. (6 sts)

Row 2: Purl.

Row 3: K1, m1, k to last st, m1, k1. (8 sts)

Row 4: Purl.

Break A and join in B.

Row 5: K1, m1, k to last st, m1, k1. (10 sts)

Row 6: Purl.

Rep rows 5–6, 7 times more. (24 sts)

Beg with a k row, work 12 rows in st st.

Bind (cast) off.

Front leg

Make 2

Cast on 6 sts in A.

Beg with a k row, work 34 rows in st st.

Work paws as for back legs from * to *.

Ear

Make 4; 2 in A and 2 in B

Cast on 6 sts.

Row 1: Inc, k to last 2 sts, inc, k1. (8 sts)

Beg with a p row, work 7 rows in st st.

Row 9: K1, skpo, k2, k2tog, k1. (6 sts)

Row 10: P2tog, p2, p2tog. (4 sts)

Row 11: Skpo, k2tog. (2 sts)

Break yarn, thread it through rem sts, and pull up securely.

Tail

Cast on 6 sts in A.

Beg with a k row, work 62 rows in st st.

Row 63: Skpo, k2, k2tog. (4 sts)

Row 64: [P2tog] twice. (2 sts)

Break yarn, thread it through rem sts, and pull up securely.

To make up

On face, using black yarn, work two small coils of chain stitch for the eyes (see page 124). Using a separated strand of beige yarn, work a few straight stitches (see page 124) on each side of the face for the whiskers.

Place the face on the head part of the main scarf so that the right sides are together. Oversew (see page 125) the side seams. Turn the head the right way out and sew the top edge in place using mattress stitch (see page 125).

Oversew the front legs in place underneath the head, where the head meets the main part of the scarf.

Place one ear piece in A and one ear piece in B right sides together and oversew around the edge, leaving the lower (cast-on) edges open for turning. Turn the ears the right way out. Using B, work a row of chain stitch around the outer edge of the ear where the two yarns meet. Oversew the ears in position.

Sew the long seam of the tail using flat stitch (see page 125) and oversew in place, just where the garter stitch border meets the main part of the scarf.

Weave in all loose ends.

pig scarf

Calling all pig lovers—and I know you're out there. Now, if you're looking for a conversation opener, this scarf is sure to fit the bill. It's knitted in a flattering shade of pink, which is a big favorite of mine. (You could knit it in another color, of course—but I don't think it would be quite the same.) With this scarf around your neck, you'd look right at home strolling around the farm, but I reckon it would look just as good on a city street.

Yarn and materials
Hayfield Chunky with Wool (80% acrylic, 20% wool) bulky (chunky) yarn
2 x 3½oz (100g) balls (159yd/145m) in shade 693 Blossom
Small amounts of black, off-white, and gray light worsted (DK) yarn
A small handful of 100% polyester toy filling

Needles and equipment
US 10½ (6.5mm) knitting needles
Yarn sewing needle
Large-eyed embroidery needle

Gauge (tension)
14 sts and 19 rows in stockinette (stocking) stitch to a 4-in (10-cm) square on US 10½ (6.5mm) needles.

Measurements
The finished scarf is 55½in (141cm) long, including back legs.

Abbreviations
See page 126.

To make scarf
Cast on 10 sts.
Row 1: Inc, k to last 2 sts, inc, k1. *(12 sts)*
Row 2: Purl.
Row 3: K1, m1, k to last st, m1, k1. *(14 sts)*
Row 4: Purl.
Rep rows 3–4, 4 times more. *(22 sts)*
Beg with a k row, work 8 rows in st st.
Row 22: Knit.
Row 23: K3, p to last 3 sts, k3.
Rep rows 22–23, 112 times.
Knit 6 rows.
Shape back legs
Row 254: K6, bind (cast) off 10 sts, k to end.
Work on 6 sts just knitted only, leaving rem sts on needle.
*Knit 7 rows.
Beg with a k row, work 8 rows in st st.
Shape trotter
Next row: Ssk, k2, k2tog. *(4 sts)*
Next row: [P2tog] twice. *(2 sts)*
Next row: K2tog. *(1 st)*
Break yarn and fasten off.**
Rejoin yarn to rem sts on WS of work.
Rep from * to **.

Face
Cast on 10 sts.
Row 1: Inc, k to last 2 sts, inc, k1. *(12 sts)*
Row 2: Purl.
Row 3: K1, m1, k to last st, m1, k1. *(14 sts)*
Row 4: Purl.
Rep rows 3–4, 4 times more. *(22 sts)*
Beg with a k row, work 8 rows in st st.
Bind (cast) off.

Ear

Make 4

Cast on 7 sts.

Beg with a k row, work 6 rows in st st.

Row 7: K1, ssk, k1, k2tog, k1. *(5 sts)*

Row 8: Purl.

Row 9: Ssk, k1, k2tog. *(3 sts)*

Row 10: P3tog. *(1 st)*

Break yarn and fasten off.

Tail

Cast on 3 sts.

Beg with a k row, work 30 rows in st st.

Row 31: Sl1, k2tog, psso. *(1 st)*

Break yarn and fasten off.

To make up

On face, using black yarn, embroider two small circles using chain stitch (see page 124) for the centers of the eyes. Work a circle of chain stitch around the eye centers using off-white yarn. Oversew the nose in position, stuffing it lightly as you go. Using gray yarn, work two straight stitches (see page 124) on the nose for the nostrils.

Place the face on the head part of the main scarf so that the right sides are together. Oversew (see page 125) the side seams. Turn the head the right way out and sew the top edge in place using mattress stitch (see page 125).

Oversew the front legs in place underneath the head, where the head meets the main part of the scarf.

Place two ear pieces right sides together and oversew around the sides, leaving the lower (cast-on) edge open for turning. Turn the right way out and sew the lower edge together using flat stitch (see page 125). Make the second ear in the same way. Oversew the ears in place using the photograph as a guide.

Tie a knot in the tail and oversew it in place on the pig's lower end, just where the garter stitch border meets the main part of the scarf.

Weave in all loose ends.

Front leg

Make 2

Cast on 6 sts.

Knit 20 rows.

Beg with a k row, work 12 rows in st st.

Shape trotter

Next row: Ssk, k2, k2tog. *(4 sts)*

Next row: [P2tog] twice. *(2 sts)*

Next row: K2tog. *(1 st)*

Break yarn and fasten off.

Nose

The nose is knitted from the bottom to the top.

Cast on 3 sts.

Row 1: [Inc] twice, k1. *(5 sts)*

Row 2: Purl.

Row 3: K1, m1, k3, m1, k1. *(7 sts)*

Row 4: Purl.

Row 5: K1, ssk, k1, k2tog, k1. *(5 sts)*

Row 6: P2tog, p1, p2tog. *(3 sts)*

Row 7: Sl1, k2tog, psso. *(1 st)*

Break yarn and fasten off.

mouse socks

A sweet pair of pink-nosed mice for two gorgeous little feet. If you're new to the world of sock knitting, these socks, knitted in a beautifully soft gray yarn, could be a great place to start, and your only problem will be prising the socks off their new owner. You will need to use a set of double-pointed needles or a short circular needle to make the socks, which can feel a little strange at first. But once you've knitted one pair of socks, like many other knitters you may well find yourself addicted.

Yarn

Sublime Baby Cashmere Merino Silk DK (75% wool, 20% silk, 5% cashmere) light worsted (DK) yarn
1 x 1¾oz (50g) ball (116yd/126m) in shade 277 Tittlemouse (A)
1 x 1¾oz (50g) ball (116yd/126m) in shade 001 Piglet (B)
Small amounts of black and beige light worsted (DK) yarn

Needles and equipment

US 8 (5mm) knitting needles
A set of 4 (or 5) US 6 (4mm) double-pointed needles (DPNs) or a US 6 (4mm) short circular needle designed for knitting socks and other smaller items (see page 122 for more information on knitting on DPNs and circular needles)
US 3 (3.25mm) knitting needles
Stitch marker or small safety pin
Yarn sewing needle
Large-eyed embroidery needle

Gauge (tension)

22 sts and 28 rows in stockinette (stocking) stitch to a 4-in (10-cm) square on US 6 (4mm) needles.

Measurements

The finished socks measure 5¾in (14.5cm) from the heel to the tip of the toe. They should fit a child's shoe size US 7–8 (UK 6–7/EU 23–24)

Abbreviations

See page 126.

To make socks

Make 2

Using US 8 (5mm) needles, cast on 32 sts in A. Transfer sts to US 6 (4mm) DPNs or circular needle and mark your first cast-on stitch with stitch marker or small safety pin.
Round 1: [K1, p1] to end.
Rep round 1, 4 times more.
Knit 22 rounds.
Shape heel back
Row 1: K8, turn. *(8 sts)*
Row 2: P16. *(16 sts)*
(If using DPNs, keep all 16 sts on one needle.)
Row 3: Sl1, k to end.
Row 4: Sl1 pwise, p to end.
Rep rows 3–4, 5 times more.
Shape heel base
Row 15: K10, ssk, k1, turn. *(15 sts)*

Row 16: Sl1 pwise, p5, p2tog, p1, turn. *(14 sts)*

Row 17: Sl1, k6, ssk, k1, turn. *(13 sts)*

Row 18: Sl1 pwise, p7, p2tog, p1, turn. *(12 sts)*

Row 19: Sl1, k8, ssk, turn. *(11 sts)*

Row 20: Sl1 pwise, p8, p2tog. *(10 sts)*

Row 21: Knit.

Shape foot

Row 22 and forming base for rounds: Knit, putting stitch marker or safety pin between 5th and 6th sts to mark back of sock. With empty needle if using DPNs, pick up and k 8 sts up first side of heel back then k across 16 sts of top part of sock. With another empty needle if using DPNs, pick up and k 8 sts down side of second heel back and then 5 sts along base of heel (to stitch marker). These 42 sts will form the foot part of the sock.

Round 1: K10, k2tog, k18, ssk, k10. *(40 sts)*

Round 2: Knit.

Round 3: K9, k2tog, k18, ssk, k9. *(38 sts)*

Round 4: Knit.

Round 5: K8, k2tog, k18, ssk, k8. *(36 sts)*

Round 6: Knit.

Round 7: K7, k2tog, k18, ssk, k7. *(34 sts)*

Round 8: Knit.

Round 9: K6, k2tog, k18, ssk, k6. *(32 sts)*

Knit 19 more rounds.

Shape toe

Round 1: K5, ssk, k2, k2tog, k10, ssk, k2, k2tog, k5. *(28 sts)*

Round 2: Knit.

Round 3: K4, ssk, k2, k2tog, k8, ssk, k2, k2tog, k4. *(24 sts)*

Round 4: Knit.

Round 5: K3, ssk, k2, k2tog, k6, ssk, k2, k2tog, k3. *(20 sts)*

Break A and join in B.

Round 6: Knit.

Round 7: K2, ssk, k2, k2tog, k4, ssk, k2, k2tog, k2. *(16 sts)*

Round 8: K1, ssk, k2, k2tog, k2, ssk, k2, k2tog, k1. *(12 sts)*

Break yarn, thread it through rem sts, and pull up securely.

Ear

Make 8; 4 in A and 4 in B

Using US 3 (3.25mm) needles, cast on 4 sts.

Row 1: [Inc, k1] twice. *(6 sts)*

Beg with a p row, work 3 rows in st st.

Row 5: K2tog, k2, ssk. *(4 sts)*

Row 6: [P2tog] twice. *(2 sts)*

Row 7: K2tog. *(1 st)*

Break yarn and fasten off.

To make up

Place one ear piece in A and one ear piece in B right sides together and oversew (see page 125) around the edge, leaving the lower (cast-on) edges open for turning. Turn the ears the right way out. Using A, work a row of chain stitch (see page 124) around the outer edge of the ear where the two yarns meet. Oversew the ears in position.

Using black yarn, work two small coils of chain stitch for the eyes. Using a separated strand of beige yarn, work a few straight stitches (see page 124) on each side of the face for the whiskers.

Weave in all loose ends.

honeycomb cowl

An utterly original take on the 1960s beehive tea cozy, this is a a super-cute, super-warm and super-fun neck warmer for little ones. It's knitted in a special cable stitch that's very easy to get the hang of. And it comes complete with its own tiny swarm of fuzzy bees that are guaranteed to be sting-free.

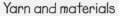

Yarn and materials
Debbie Bliss Rialto Chunky (100% wool) bulky
(chunky) yarn
1 x 1¾oz (50g) ball (66yd/60m) in shade 007 Gold (A)
Sirdar Country Style (40% nylon, 30% wool, 30% acrylic)
light worsted (DK) yarn
1 x 1¾oz (50g) ball (170yd/155m) in shade 0417 Black (B)
1 x 1¾oz (50g) ball (170yd/155m) in shade 0612 Maple (C)
Wendy Air (70% kid mohair, 30% nylon) lace weight yarn
1 x ¾oz (25g) ball (219yd/200m) in shade 2612
Lottie (D)
A handful of 100% polyester toy filling

Needles and equipment
US 10½ (6.5mm) knitting needles
Medium size cable needle
US 3 (3.25mm) knitting needles
Yarn sewing needle

Gauge (tension)
15 sts and 21 rows in stockinette (stocking) stitch to a
4-in (10-cm) square on US 10½ (6.5mm) needles.

Measurements
The finished cowl is 15½in (39cm) in circumference and
is 5in (13cm) deep. It should fit an average size child of
2–4 years.

Abbreviations
See page 126.

To make cowl
Using US 10½ (6.5mm) needles, cast on 62 sts in A.
Row 1: Knit.
*Beg with a p row, work 3 rows in st st.
Row 5: K1, [C3R, C3L] to last st, k1.
Beg with a p row, work 3 rows st st, beg with a p row.
Row 9: K1, [C3L, C3R] to last st, k1.**
Rep from * to ** twice more.
Beg with a p row, work 3 rows in st st.
Bind (cast) off.

To make bees
Make 3 bees for the cowl—and a few extra if you like.
Using US 3 (3.25mm) needles, cast on 3 sts in B.
Row 1: [Inc] 3 times. *(6 sts)*
Row 2: Knit.
Leave B at side of work and join in C.
Row 3: K1, m1, k4, m1, k1. *(8 sts)*
Row 4: Knit.
Leave C at side of work and join in B.
Knit 2 rows.
Leave B at side of work and join in C.
Knit 2 rows.
Break C and work remainder of bee in B.

Row 9: Skpo, k4, k2tog. *(6 sts)*
Row 10: Skpo, k2, k2tog. *(4 sts)*
Break yarn, thread it through rem sts, and pull up securely.

Wings
Using US 3 (3.25mm) needles, cast on 3 sts in D.
Row 1: [Inc] 3 times. *(6 sts)*
Knit 5 rows.
Row 6: [K2tog] 3 times. *(3 sts)*
Break yarn, thread it through rem sts, and pull up securely.

To make up
Join the short edges of the cowl using flat stitch (see page 125).
Join the seam of the body of each bee using mattress stitch (see page 125), stuffing lightly with polyester toy filling as you work. For the wings, thread the yarn tail that you threaded through final stitches down one side of the piece, to the center. Gather the piece in the center to make two wings and sew to the back of each bee. Sew the bees to the cowl.
Weave in all loose ends.

CHAPTER 2
furry friends

Calling pet lovers everywhere—stop what you're doing, pick up your yarn and needles, and get clicking. Knit the animal creations on the following few pages in the colors I've used, or choose your own combinations to knit a wooly version of your beloved family pet or favorite garden visitor.

fox scarf

For that vintage pin-up look, whip yourself up this animal-friendly version of the classic fox stole. Wear him around your neck and let him dangle. Or wind him so his face and front legs are at the front and his back legs and lovely bushy tail hang down the back. I've knitted this big-eared beauty in a stunning shade of auburn—but if gray is more your thing, I think it would look just as great in that color too. Or you could just knit a pair of foxes…

Yarn

Wendy Serenity Chunky (70% acrylic, 20% alpaca, 10% wool) bulky (chunky) yarn
2 x 3½oz (100g) balls (87yd/80m) in shade 3210 Auburn (A)
Katia Peru (40% wool, 40% acrylic, 20% alpaca) bulky (chunky) yarn
1 x 3½oz (100g) ball (115yd/106m) in shade 002 (B)
Bergere de France Merinos Alpaga (60% merino, 40% alpaca) bulky (chunky) yarn
1 x 1¾oz (50g) ball (71yd/65m) in shade 29899 Ecru (C)
Small amounts of black and off-white light worsted (DK) yarn

Needles and equipment

US 10½ (6.5mm) knitting needles
Yarn sewing needle
Large-eyed embroidery needle

Gauge (tension)

14 sts and 20 rows in stockinette (stocking) stitch to a 4-in (10-cm) square on US 10½ (6.5mm) needles using A.

Measurements

The finished scarf is 50in (127cm) long, including the back legs.

Abbreviations

See page 126.

To make scarf

Cast on 2 sts in A.
Row 1: [Inc] twice. *(4 sts)*
Row 2: Purl.
Row 3: K1, m1, k2, m1, k1. *(6 sts)*
Row 4: Purl.
Row 5: K1, m1, k to last st, m1, k1. *(8 sts)*
Row 6: Purl.
Rep rows 5–6, 8 times more. *(24 sts)*
Beg with a k row, work 7 rows in st st.
Row 30: Knit.
Row 31: K3, p to last 3 sts, k3.
Rep rows 30–31, 95 times more.
Knit 6 rows.
Shape back legs
Row 228: K7, bind (cast) off 10 sts, k to end.
Turn and work on group of 7 sts just knitted only, leaving rem sts on needle.
*Knit 11 rows.
Break A and join in B.
Knit 16 rows.
Shape paw
Next row: K1, k2tog, k1, ssk, k1. *(5 sts)*
Next row: K2tog, k1, ssk. *(3 sts)*
Next row: Sl1, k2tog, psso. *(1 st)*
Break yarn and fasten off.
With WS of main body facing, rejoin A to rem 7 sts.
Work from * to end.

Front leg

Make 2
Using A, cast on 7 sts.
Knit 26 rows.
Break A and work remainder of leg in B.
Knit 24 rows.

Shape paw
Next row: K1, k2tog, k1, ssk, k1. *(5 sts)*
Next row: K2tog, k1, ssk. *(3 sts)*
Next row: Sl1, k2tog, psso. *(1 st)*
Break yarn and fasten off.

Face

Cast on 2 sts in A.
Row 1: [Inc] twice. *(4 sts)*
Row 2: Purl.
Row 3: K1, m1, k2, m1, k1. *(6 sts)*
Row 4: Purl.
Row 5: K1, m1, k to last st, m1, k1.
(8 sts)
Row 6: Purl.
Rep rows 5–6, 8 times more. *(24 sts)*
Beg with a k row, work 7 rows in st st.
Bind (cast) off.

Ear

Make 2
Cast on 12 sts in A.
Beg with a k row, work 2 rows in st st.
Row 3: K1, ssk, k6, k2tog, k1. *(10 sts)*
Row 4: Purl.
Row 5: K1, ssk, k4, k2tog, k1. *(8 sts)*
Row 6: Purl.
Row 7: K1, ssk, k2, k2tog, k1. *(6 sts)*
Row 8: Purl.
Row 9: K1, ssk, k2tog, k1. *(4 sts)*
Row 10: [P2tog] twice. *(2 sts)*
Row 11: K2tog. *(1 st)*
Row 12: Inc pwise. *(2 sts)*
Row 13: [Inc] twice. *(4 sts)*
Row 14: Purl.
Row 15: K1, m1, k2, m1, k1. *(6 sts)*
Row 16: Purl.
Row 17: K1, m1, k4, m1, k1. *(8 sts)*
Row 18: Purl.
Row 19: K1, m1, k6, m1, k1. *(10 sts)*
Row 20: Purl.
Row 21: K1, m1, k8, m1, k1. *(12 sts)*
Beg with a p row, work 2 rows in st st.
Bind (cast) off kwise.

Tail

Cast on 8 sts in A.
Row 1: Inc, k to last 2 sts, inc, k1.
(10 sts)
Beg with a p row, work 3 rows in st st.
Row 5: K2, m1, k to last 2 sts, m1, k2.
(12 sts)
Beg with a p row, work 3 rows in st st.

Row 67: K1, [ssk] twice, [k2tog] twice, k1. *(6 sts)*
Row 68: P2tog, p2, p2tog. *(4 sts)*
Break yarn, thread it through rem sts, and pull up securely.

To make up

On face, using black light worsted (DK) yarn, work two small coils of black chain stitch (see page 124) for the centers of the eyes. Using off-white light worsted (DK) yarn, work a circle of chain stitch around the eye centers. Using black light worsted (DK) yarn, work a coil of chain stitch for the nose. Using the same yarn, work three straight stitches (see page 124) above each eye for the lashes.

Place the face on the head part of the main scarf so that the right sides are together. Oversew the side seams (see page 125). Turn the head the right way out and sew the top edge in place using mattress stitch (see page 125).

Sew the seam of the black part of the back legs using flat stitch (see page 125), continuing ¾in (2cm) into the auburn part of the leg. Sew the seam of the black part of the front legs using flat stitch, continuing 2in (5cm) into the auburn part of the leg. Oversew the front legs in place underneath the head, where the head meets the main part of the scarf. Fold the ears so that the right side of the front and back pieces are together and oversew the two sides. Turn the right way out and sew the lower edge together using flat stitch. Oversew the ears in place.

Sew the back seam of the tail using flat stitch and matching yarns. Oversew the tail in place in the center of the fox's lower end, just where the garter stitch border meets the main part of the scarf.

Weave in all loose ends.

Row 9: K3, m1, k to last 3 sts, m1, k3. *(14 sts)*
Beg with a p row, work 3 rows in st st.
Row 13: K4, m1, k to last 4 sts, m1, k4. *(16 sts)*
Beg with a p row, work 3 rows in st st.
Rep last 4 rows once more. *(18 sts)*
Row 21: K5, m1, k to last 5 sts, m1, k5. *(20 sts)*
Beg with a p row, work 3 rows in st st.
Rep last 4 rows once more. *(22 sts)*
Row 29: K6, m1, k to last 6 sts, m1, k6. *(24 sts)*
Beg with a p row, work 3 rows in st st.
Rep last 4 rows once more. *(26 sts)*
Beg with a k row, work 6 rows in st st.
Row 43: K6, ssk, k10, k2tog, k6. *(24 sts)*
Beg with a p row, work 3 rows in st st.
Row 47: K5, ssk, k10, k2tog, k5. *(22 sts)*
Beg with a p row, work 3 rows in st st.
Row 51: K5, ssk, k8, k2tog, k5. *(20 sts)*
Row 52: Purl.
Break A and join in C. Work remainder of tail in C.
Row 53: Knit.
Row 54: Purl.
Row 55: K4, ssk, k8, k2tog, k4. *(18 sts)*
Beg with a p row, work 3 rows in st st.
Row 59: K4, ssk, k6, k2tog, k4. *(16 sts)*
Row 60: Purl.
Row 61: K3, ssk, k6, k2tog, k3. *(14 sts)*
Row 62: Purl.
Row 63: K3, ssk, k4, k2tog, k3. *(12 sts)*
Row 64: Purl.
Row 65: K2, ssk, k4, k2tog, k2. *(10 sts)*
Row 66: Purl.

rabbit scarf

Downright charming but not over-cute—that's the verdict for this big bunny-rabbit scarf. It's generous enough to fit teens—and those whose teenage years are a fading memory, but who don't see why they should be left out of the craze for all things woodland. Because it's knitted in a super-chunky yarn, you'll find the scarf grows really quickly, so it should be one of the fastest projects in the whole book to complete and make your own.

Yarn
Lion Brand Wool-Ease Thick & Quick (80% acrylic, 20% wool) super-bulky (super-chunky) yarn
2 x 6oz (170g) balls (108yd/98m) in shade 098 Linen (A)
Sirdar Big Softie (51% wool, 49% acrylic) super-bulky (super-chunky) yarn
1 x 1¾oz (50g) ball (49yd/45m) in shade 330 Meringue (B)
Small amounts of black and white light worsted (DK) yarn

Needles and equipment
US 13 (9mm) knitting needles
Yarn sewing needle
Large-eyed embroidery needle
A pompom maker to make 4½in (11.5cm) pompoms, or two cardboard circles each measuring 4½in (11.5cm) in diameter with a 2¼in (5.5cm) diameter hole in the center

Gauge (tension)
9 sts and 12 rows in stockinette (stocking) stitch to a 4-in (10-cm) square on US 13 (9mm) needles using A.

Measurements
The finished scarf is 62½in (159cm) long, including the back legs.

Abbreviations
See page 126.

To make scarf
Cast on 12 sts in A.
Row 1: Knit.
Row 2: Purl
Row 3: Inc, k to last 2 sts, inc, k1. *(14 sts)*
Row 4: Purl.
Rep rows 1–4 once more. *(16 sts)*
Row 9: Inc, k to last 2 sts, inc, k1. *(18 sts)*
Row 10: Purl.
Rep rows 9–10 once more. *(20 sts)*
Beg with a k row, work 6 rows in st st.
Row 19: Knit.
Row 20: Knit.
Row 21: K3, p to last 3 sts, k3.
Rep rows 20–21, 75 times more.
Knit 6 rows.

Shape back legs
Row 177: K5, bind (cast) off 10 sts, k to end.
Cont working on 5 sts just worked only, leaving rem sts on needle.
*Knit 7 rows.
Break A and join in B.
Beg with a k row, work 12 rows in st st.
Shape paw
Next row: Ssk, k1, k2tog. *(3 sts)*
Next row: P3tog. *(1 st)*
Break yarn and fasten off.**
Rejoin A to second group of 5 sts on WS of work.
Rep from * to ** once.

Front leg
Make 2
Cast on 5 sts in A.
Knit 12 rows.
Break A and join in B.
Work 14 rows in st st.
Shape paw
Row 27: Ssk, k1, k2tog. *(3 sts)*
Break yarn, thread it through rem sts, and pull up securely.

Face
Cast on 12 sts in A.
Row 1: Knit.
Row 2: Purl
Row 3: Inc, k to last 2 sts, inc, k1. *(14 sts)*
Row 4: Purl.
Rep rows 1–4 once more. *(16 sts)*
Row 9: Inc, k to last 2 sts, inc, k1. *(18 sts)*
Row 10: Purl.
Rep rows 9–10 once more. *(20 sts)*
Beg with a k row, work 6 rows in st st.
Bind (cast) off.

Ear
Make 2
Cast on 4 sts in A.
Beg with a k row, work 12 rows in st st.
Row 13: Ssk, k2tog. *(2 sts)*
Row 14: [Inc pwise] twice. *(4 sts)*
Beg with a k row, work 12 rows in st st.
Bind (cast) off.

To make up
For face, using black yarn, embroider two small circles using chain stitch (see page 124) for the centers of the eyes. Using white yarn, work a circle of chain stitch around the eye centers. For the lashes, use a separated strand of black yarn to work three straight stitches (see page 124) above each eye. Using black yarn, work a chain stitch cross for the nose. Place the face on the head part of the main scarf so that the right sides are together. Oversew the side seams (see page 125). Turn the head the right way out and sew the top edge in place using mattress stitch (see page 125).
Oversew the front legs in place underneath the head, where the head meets the main part of the scarf.
Fold the ears in half so that the right sides are on the outside and oversew the sides and lower edge. Oversew the ears in place at the top of the head using the photograph as a guide. Using a single stitch, join the back part of the ear to the side of the scarf, to make the ears stand up.
For the tail, make a pompom, using the pompom maker or cardboard circles, using B. Sew the pompom in place just above the garter stitch border at the lower end of the scarf. Weave in all loose ends.

tabby cat scarf

If you're the sort of person who loves that cozy feeling of a cat wrapped around your neck, then look no further. This is the perfect scarf for you. It's knitted in a chunky yarn, in straightforward stockinette (stocking) stitch, so you'll find it grows pretty quickly. And the stripes are just enough work to keep you on your toes. The scarf is very simple to customize. So if you, or the lucky scarf recipient, have a white cat, choose white or cream yarn. And for a marmalade cat, knit in shades of rust and coral.

Yarn
Sirdar Click Chunky with Wool (70% acrylic, 30% wool) bulky (chunky) yarn
2 x 1¾oz (50g) balls (81yd/75m) in shade 119 Flinty (A)
2 x 1¾oz (50g) balls (81yd/75m) in shade 185 Gull Grey (B)
Small amounts of black and off-white light worsted (DK) yarn

Needles and equipment
US 10½ (6.5mm) knitting needles
Yarn sewing needle
Large-eyed embroidery needle

Gauge (tension)
14 sts and 19 rows in stockinette (stocking) stitch to a 4-in (10-cm) square on US 10½ (6.5mm) needles.

Measurements
The finished scarf is 50in (127cm) long, including the back legs.

Abbreviations
See page 126.

To make scarf
Cast on 18 sts in A.
Row 1: Inc, k to last 2 sts, inc, k1. *(20 sts)*
Row 2: Purl.
Row 3: K1, m1, k to last st, m1, k1. *(22 sts)*
Row 4: Purl.
Rep last 2 rows once more. *(24 sts)*
Beg with a k row, work 21 rows in st st.
Leave A at side of work and join in B.
Row 28: Knit.
Row 29: K3, p to last 3 sts, k3.
Rep rows 28–29 once more, carrying A up side of work at beg of row 30.
Leave B at side of work and use A.
Row 32: Knit.
Row 33: K3, p to last 3 sts, k3.
Rep rows 32–33 once more, carrying B up side of work at beg of row 34.
Rep rows rows 28–35 (last 8 rows), 23 times more.
Cont in A, knit 6 rows.
Shape back legs
Row 226: K6, bind (cast) off 12 sts, k to end.
Cont on 6 sts just knitted only, leaving rem sts on needle.
Knit 11 rows.
Change to B.
Knit 8 rows.
Shape paw
Next row: K2, turn and work on 2 sts just worked only.
*Knit 3 rows.
Next row: Bind (cast) off 1 st, [pick up and k 1 st from row ends, bind (cast) off 1 st] twice, k next st on needle, bind (cast) off 1 st, k1.** *(2 sts)*
Rep from * to ** once more.
Knit 3 rows.
Bind (cast) off 1 st [pick up and k 1 st from row ends, bind (cast) off 1 st] twice.
Break yarn and fasten off.
Rejoin A to rem 6 sts on WS of work.

Knit 11 rows.
Change to B.
Knit 8 rows.
Shape paw as for first back leg.

Front leg

Make 2

Cast on 6 sts in A.
Knit 38 rows.
Change to B.
Knit 8 rows.
Shape paw as for back legs.

Face

Cast on 18 sts in A.
Row 1: Inc, k to last 2 sts, inc, k1. *(20 sts)*
Row 2: Purl.
Row 3: K1, m1, k to last st, m1, k1. *(22 sts)*
Row 4: Purl.
Rep last 2 rows once more. *(24 sts)*
Beg with a k row, work 20 rows in st st.
Bind (cast) off.

Ear

Make 2

Cast on 10 sts in A.
Beg with a k row, work 2 rows in st st.
Row 3: K1, ssk, k4, k2tog, k1. *(8 sts)*
Row 4: Purl.
Row 5: K1, ssk, k2, k2tog, k1. *(6 sts)*
Row 6: Purl.
Row 7: K1, ssk, k2tog, k1. *(4 sts)*
Row 8: [P2tog] twice. *(2 sts)*
Row 9: K2tog. *(1 st)*
Row 10: Inc pwise. *(2 sts)*
Row 11: [Inc] twice. *(4 sts)*
Row 12: Purl.
Row 13: K1, m1, k2, m1, k1. *(6 sts)*
Row 14: Purl.
Row 15: K1, m1, k4, m1, k1. *(8 sts)*
Row 16: Purl.
Row 17: K1, m1, k6, m1, k1. *(10 sts)*
Beg with a p row, work 2 rows in st st.
Bind (cast) off kwise.

Tail

Cast on 11 sts in B.
Beg with a k row, work 32 rows in st st.
Row 33: Ssk, k7, k2tog. *(9 sts)*
Beg with a p row, work 9 rows in st st.
Leave B at side of work and join in A.
Beg with a k row, work 2 rows in st st.

Leave A at side of work and join in B.
Beg with a k row, work 2 rows in st st.
Rep last 4 rows in two-row stripe patt as set.
Break B and work remainder of tail in A.
Beg with a k row, work 8 rows in st st.
Next row: Ssk, k5, k2tog. *(7 sts)*
Next row: Purl.
Break yarn, thread it through rem sts, and pull up securely.

To make up

On face, using black yarn, embroider two small circles using chain stitch (see page 124) for the centers of the eyes. Work two rows of chain stitch around these circles using off-white yarn. Using black yarn, work a triangle shape in chain stitch for the nose and work a line of chain stitch from the base of the nose to the lower edge of the face. Separate a length of B into two thinner strands and use them to embroider the whiskers in backstitch.

Place the face on the head part of the main scarf so that the right sides are together. Oversew the side seams (see page 125). Turn the head the right way out and sew the top edge in place using mattress stitch (see page 125).

Oversew the front legs in place underneath the head, where the head meets the main part of the scarf. Fold the ears so that the right side of the front and back pieces are together and oversew the two sides. Turn the right way out and sew the lower edge together using flat stitch (see page 125). Oversew the ears in place using the photograph as a guide. Sew the back seam of the tail using flat stitch. Oversew the tail in place in the center of the cat's lower end, just where the garter stitch border meets the main part of the scarf. Weave in all loose ends.

marmalade kitten socks

Cute as a kitten? You certainly will be in these socks. Knitted in pure merino in two gorgeous shades of orange, I've made marmalade kitten socks. But if you prefer a gray and white, or just something plain, it's entirely up to you. These socks are knitted in the round on double-pointed needles or a circular needle. So it's not a project for complete beginners, but if you've mastered the art of knitting in the round, these would make an ideal second or third project.

Yarn
Patons Merino Extrafine DK (100% wool) light worsted (DK) yarn
1 x 1¾oz (50g) ball (131yd/120m) in shade 00125 Orange (A)
1 x 1¾oz (50g) ball (131yd/120m) in shade 00123 Apricot (B)
Small amounts of black, cream or off-white, and gray light worsted (DK) yarn

Needles and equipment
US 8 (5mm) knitting needles
A set of 4 (or 5) US 6 (4mm) double-pointed needles (DPNs) or a US 6 (4mm) short circular needle designed for knitting socks and other smaller items (see page 122 for more information on knitting on DPNs and circular needles)
Stitch marker or small safety pin
US 2/3 (3mm) knitting needles
Yarn sewing needle

Gauge (tension)
22 sts and 30 rows in stockinette (stocking) stitch to a 4-in (10-cm) square on US 6 (4mm) needles.

Measurements
The finished socks measure 6¾in (17cm) from the heel to the tip of the toe. They should fit a child's shoe size US 11½–12½ (UK 10½–11½/EU 29–30)

Abbreviations
See page 126.

To make socks
Make 2

Using US 8 (5mm) needles, cast on 40 sts in A. Transfer sts to DPNs or circular needle and mark your first cast-on stitch with stitch marker or small safety pin.

Round 1: [K2, p2] to end.
Rep round 1, 4 times more.
Round 6: Knit.
Leave A on inside of work and join in B.
Knit 2 rounds.
Leave B on inside of work and use A.
Knit 2 rounds.
Rep rounds 7–10 (the last 4 rounds), 5 times more.

Shape heel back
Break B and work heel in A only.
Row 1: K10, turn. *(10 sts)*
Row 2: P20. *(20 sts)*
(If using DPNs, keep all 20 sts on one needle.)
Row 3: Sl1, k1 to end.
Row 4: Sl1 pwise, p to end.
Rep rows 3–4, 8 times more.

Shape heel base
Row 21: K12, ssk, k1, turn. *(19 sts)*
Row 22: Sl1 pwise, p5, p2tog, p1, turn. *(18 sts)*
Row 23: Sl1, k6, ssk, k1, turn. *(17 sts)*
Row 24: Sl1 pwise, p7, p2tog, p1, turn. *(16 sts)*
Row 25: Sl1, k8, ssk, k1, turn. *(15 sts)*
Row 26: Sl1 pwise, p9, p2tog, p1, turn. *(14 sts)*
Row 27: Sl1, k10, ssk, turn. *(13 sts)*
Row 28: Sl1 pwise, p10, p2tog, turn. *(12 sts)*

Shape foot
Break A and join in B.
Row 29 and forming base for rounds: Knit, putting stitch marker or safety pin between 6th and 7th sts to mark back of sock. With empty needle if using DPNs, pick up and k 10 sts up first side of heel back then k across 20 sts of top part of sock.

Round 5: K5, ssk, k2, k2tog, k10, ssk, k2, k2tog, k5. *(28 sts)*
Round 5: K5, ssk, k2, k2tog, k10, ssk, k2, k2tog, k5. *(28 sts)*
Round 6: Knit.
Round 7: K4, ssk, k2, k2tog, k8, ssk, k2, k2tog, k4. *(24 sts)*
Round 8: Knit.
Round 9: K3, ssk, k2, k2tog, k6, ssk, k2, k2tog, k3. *(20 sts)*
Round 10: K2, ssk, k2, k2tog, k4, ssk, k2, k2tog, k2. *(16 sts)*
Round 11: K1, ssk, k2, k2tog, k2, ssk, k2, k2tog, k1. *(12 sts)*
Break yarn, thread it through rem sts, and pull up securely.

Ear

Make 8
Cast on 6 sts in A.
Beg with a k row, work 4 rows in st st.
Row 5: Skpo, k2, k2tog. *(4 sts)*
Row 6: [P2tog] twice. *(2 sts)*
Row 7: Skpo. *(1 st)*
Break yarn and fasten off.

To make up

For the ears, place two pieces together so that the right sides are on the inside. Oversew (see page 125) around the two sides, close to the edge, leaving the lower (cast-on) edge open for turning. Turn the piece the right way out and oversew the lower edge. Piece the other ears together in the same way.

For face, using black yarn, work a small coil of chain stitch (see page 124) for the centers of the eyes. Using cream yarn, work a circle of chain stitch around the eye centers. Using black yarn, work a coil of chain stitch for the nose and work a short vertical line in backstitch) from the base of the nose. Using gray yarn, work a few long straight stitches (see page 124) at the side of the nose for the whiskers.

Oversew the ears in place using the photograph as a guide. Weave in all loose ends.

With another empty needle if using DPNs, pick up and k 10 sts down side of second heel back and then k 6 sts along base of heel (to stitch marker). These 52 sts will form the foot part of the sock.
Round 1: K13, k2tog, k22, ssk, k13. *(50 sts)*
Leave B on inside of work and use A.
Round 2: Knit.
Round 3: K12, k2tog, k22, ssk, k12. *(48 sts)*
Leave A on inside of work and use B.
Round 4: Knit.
Round 5: K11, k2tog, k22, ssk, k11. *(46 sts)*
Leave B on inside of work and use A.
Round 6: Knit.
Round 7: K10, k2tog, k22, ssk, k10. *(44 sts)*
Leave A on inside of work and use B.
Round 8: Knit.
Round 9: K9, k2tog, k22, ssk, k9. *(42 sts)*
Leave B on inside of work and use A.
Round 10: Knit.
Round 11: K8, k2tog, k22, ssk, k8. *(40 sts)*
Work 22 more rounds, keeping to the striped pattern and ending with two rounds in B.
Round 34: Using A, knit.
Round 35: Using A, purl.
Break A and work remainder of sock in B.
Shape toe
Round 1: K7, ssk, k2, k2tog, k14, ssk, k2, k2tog, k7. *(36 sts)*
Round 2: Knit.
Round 3: K6, ssk, k2, k2tog, k12, ssk, k2, k2tog, k6. *(32 sts)*
Round 4: Knit.

here's a tip *When you are embroidering features onto socks, take good care to weave all the ends of the embroidery yarns firmly into the back of the stitches to prevent little toes getting caught on loops.*

dog scarf

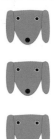

If you're a dog lover and want to show your love for all things canine, this doggie scarf is a must-have project. With its long body and little legs, the comical dachshund was just begging to be immortalized in a scarf… so here it is. I've knitted this one in chestnut brown and given him a golden trim around the chops. But for something a little simpler, you could always stick to just one color. Go brown, go gray, or go whacky and choose something bright.

Yarn
Sirdar Click Chunky (70% acrylic, 30% wool) bulky (chunky) yarn
1 x 1¾oz (50g) ball (82yd/75m) in shade 205 Fudge (A)
Hayfield Chunky with Wool (80% acrylic, 20% wool) bulky (chunky) yarn
2 x 3½oz (100g) balls (159yd/145m) in shade 695 Roasted (B)
Small amounts of black and off-white light worsted (DK) yarn

Needles and equipment
US 10½ (6.5mm) knitting needles
Yarn sewing needle
Large-eyed embroidery needle

Gauge (tension)
14 sts and 19 rows in stockinette (stocking) stitch to a 4-in (10-cm) square on US 10½ (6.5mm) needles in main yarn.

Measurements
The finished scarf is 56in (142cm) long, including back legs.

Abbreviations
See page 126.

To make scarf
Cast on 4 sts in A.
Row 1: Inc, k1, inc, k1. *(6 sts)*
Row 2: Purl.
Row 3: K1, m1, k to last st, m1, k1. *(8 sts)*
Row 4: Purl.
Rep last 2 rows, 7 times more. *(22 sts)*
Beg with a k row, work 10 rows st st.
Row 29: Knit.
Break A and join in B.
Row 30: Knit.
Row 31: K3, p to last 3 sts, k3.
Rep last 2 rows 104 times more.
Knit 6 rows.

Shape back legs
Row 246: K8, bind (cast) off 6 sts, k to end.
Work on 8 sts just worked only, leaving rem sts on needle.
*Beg with a p row, work 11 rows of st st.
Break B and join in A.
Beg with a k row, work 8 rows of st st.
Shape paw
Next row: K1, ssk, k2, k2tog, k1. *(6 sts)*
Next row: P2tog, p2, p2tog. *(4 sts)*
Next row: Ssk, k2tog. *(2 sts)*
Next row: P2tog. *(1 st)*
Break yarn and fasten off.**
Rejoin B to rem 8 sts on WS of work.
Rep from * to **.

Front leg
Make 2
Cast on 8 sts in B.
Beg with a k row, work 18 rows in st st.
Break B and join in A.
Beg with a k row, work 8 rows in st st.
Shape paw
Row 27: Ssk, k4, k2tog. *(6 sts)*
Row 28: P2tog, p2, p2tog. *(4 sts)*
Row 29: Ssk, k2tog. *(2 sts)*
Row 30: P2tog. *(1 st)*
Break yarn and fasten off.

Face
Cast on 4 sts in A.
Row 1: Inc, k1, inc, k1. *(6 sts)*
Row 2: Purl.
Row 3: K1, m1, k to last st, m1, k1. *(8 sts)*
Row 4: Purl.
Rep rows 3–4 once more. *(10 sts)*
Row 7: K1, m1, k2 in A; join in B and k4; k2, m1, k1 in A (using yarn end from ball center). *(12 sts)*
Row 8: P4 in A; p4 in B; p4 in A.
Row 9: K1, m1, k2 in A; k6 in B; k2, m1, k1 in A. *(14 sts)*
Row 10: P4 in A; p6 in A; p4 in B.
Row 11: K1, m1, k2 in A; k8 in B; k2, m1, k1 in A. *(16 sts)*
Row 12: P4 in A; p8 in B; p4 in A.
Row 13: K1, m1, k2 in A; k10 in B; k2, m1, k1 in A. *(18 sts)*
Row 14: P3 in A; p12 in B; p3 in A.
Row 15: K1, m1, k1 in A; k14 in B; k1, m1, k1 in A. *(20 sts)*
Row 16: P2 in A; p16 in B; p2 in A.
Row 17: K1, m1 in A; k18 in B; m1, k1 in A. *(22 sts)*
Row 18: P1 in A; p20 in B; p1 in A.
Break A and work remainder of face in B.
Beg with a k row, work 10 rows in st st.
Bind (cast) off.

Ear
Make 2
Cast on 8 sts in B.
Row 1: Knit.
Row 2: K1, p to last st, k1.
Rep rows 1–2, 9 times more.
Row 21: K1, ssk, k2, k2tog, k1. *(6 sts)*
Row 22: K1, p4, k1.
Row 23: Ssk, k2, k2tog. *(4 sts)*
Row 24: [P2tog] twice. *(2 sts)*
Row 25: Skpo. *(1 st)*
Break yarn and fasten off.

Tail
Cast on 8 sts in B.
Beg with a k row, work 8 rows in st st.
Row 9: K1, ssk, k2, k2tog, k1. *(6 sts)*
Beg with a p row, work 3 rows in st st.
Row 13: Ssk, k2, k2tog. *(4 sts)*
Row 14: Purl.
Row 15: Ssk, k2tog. *(2 sts)*
Row 16: P2tog. *(1 st)*
Break yarn and fasten off.

To make up
For face, using black yarn, embroider two small circles using chain stitch (see page 124) for the centers of the eyes. Using white yarn, work a circle of chain stitch around the eye centers. Using black yarn, work an oval shape in chain stitch for the nose.
Place the face down on the head part of the main scarf so that the right sides are together. Oversew the side seams (see page 125). Turn the head the right way out and sew the top edge in place using mattress stitch (see page 125). Oversew the front legs in place underneath the head, where the head meets the main part of the scarf.
Oversew the ears in place at the top of the head using the photograph as a guide.
Sew the back seam of the tail using flat stitch (see page 125). Oversew the tail in place in the center of the dog's lower end, just where the garter stitch border meets the main part of the scarf.
Weave in all loose ends.

fox mitts

Everyone loves the look of a slinky red fox. Their hunting and feeding habits aren't always appreciated—but with these fox mittens, you don't have to worry about that. The yarn used in the mittens is mostly from alpaca, so as well as keeping little hands cozy, it's incredibly light, and very nice to work with.

Yarn

UK Alpaca Super Fine DK (70% alpaca, 30% wool) light worsted (DK) yarn

1 x 1¾oz (50g) ball (122yd/112m) in shade 14 Rust (A)

1 x 1¾oz (50g) ball (122yd/112m) in shade 01 Parchment (B)

Small amounts of black and off-white light worsted (DK) yarn

Needles and equipment

US 6 (4mm) knitting needles

US 3 (3.25mm) knitting needles

Stitch holder

Yarn sewing needle

Large-eyed embroidery needle

Gauge (tension)

20 sts and 28 rows in stockinette (stocking) stitch to a 4-in (10-cm) square on US 6 (4mm) needles.

Measurements

The finished mittens measure 7½in (19cm) from the base of the wrist to the tip and should fit an average size child of 7–10 years.

Abbreviations

See page 126.

Right mitten

Using US 6 (4mm) needles, cast on 36 sts in A.

Row 1: [K2, p2] to end.

Rep row 1, 13 times more.

Beg with a k row, work 4 rows in st st.*

Row 19: K22, [inc] twice, k to end. *(38 sts)*

Row 20: Purl.

Row 21: Knit.

Row 22: P12, inc pwise, p2, inc pwise, p to end. *(40 sts)*

Row 23: Knit.

Row 24: Purl.

Row 25: K22, inc, k4, inc, k to end. *(42 sts)*

Row 26: Purl.

Row 27: Knit.

Row 28: P12, inc pwise, p6, inc pwise, p to end. *(44 sts)*

Row 29: Knit.

Row 30: Purl.

Row 31: K22, inc, k8, inc, k to end. *(46 sts)*

Row 32: Purl.

Row 33: Knit.

Row 34: P12, inc pwise, p10, inc pwise, p to end. *(48 sts)*

Row 35: K23, put next 12 sts onto stitch holder, k to end. *(36 sts)*

Cont on 36 sts on main needles only.

Beg with a p row, work 9 rows in st st.

Break A and join in B.

Row 45: K8 in B; rejoin A and k7; k in B to end, using yarn from ball center.

Row 46: P22 in B; p5 in A; p in B to end.

Row 47: K1, skpo, k7 in B; k3 in A; k6, k2tog, k2, skpo, k8, k2tog, k1 in B. *(32 sts)*

Row 48: P1, p2tog, p6, p2togtbl, p2, p2tog, p6 in B; p1 in A; p7, p2togtbl, p1 in B. *(28 sts)*

Break A and the strand of B currently at the center of the piece and use other strand of B.

Row 49: K1, skpo, k12, k2tog, k2, skpo, k4, k2tog, k1. *(24 sts)*

Row 50: P1, p2tog, p2, p2togtbl, p2, p2tog, p10, p2togtbl, p1. *(20 sts)*

Row 51: K1, skpo, k8, k2tog, k2, skpo, k2tog, k1. *(16 sts)*

Row 52: P1, p2tog, p2togtbl, p2tog, p6, p2tog, p1. *(12 sts)*

Break yarn, thread it through rem sts, and pull up securely.
Work thumb
With RS facing you, rejoin A to 12 sts on stitch holder.
Beg with a k row, work 8 rows in st st.
Next row: K1, [k2tog, k2] twice, k2tog, k1. *(9 sts)*
Next row: Purl.
Next row: [K1, k2tog] 3 times. *(6 sts)*
Break yarn, thread it through rem sts, and pull up securely.

Left mitten
Rows 1–18: Work as for right mitten to *.
Row 19: K12, [inc] twice, k to end. *(38 sts)*
Row 20: Purl.
Row 21: Knit.
Row 22: P22, inc pwise, p2, inc pwise, p to end. *(40 sts)*
Row 23: Knit.
Row 24: Purl.
Row 25: K12, inc, k4, inc, k to end. *(42 sts)*
Row 26: Purl.
Row 27: Knit.
Row 28: P22, inc pwise, p6, inc pwise, p to end. *(44 sts)*
Row 29: Knit.
Row 30: Purl.
Row 31: K12, inc, k8, inc, k to end. *(46 sts)*
Row 32: Purl.
Row 33: Knit.
Row 34: P22, inc pwise, p10, inc pwise, p to end. *(48 sts)*
Row 35: K13, put next 12 sts onto stitch holder, k to end. *(36 sts)*
Cont on 36 sts on main needles only.
Beg with a p row, work 9 rows in st st.
Break A and join in B.
Row 45: K21 in B; rejoin A and k7; k in B to end, using yarn from ball center.

Row 46: P9 in B, p5 in A, p in B to end.
Row 47: K1, skpo, k8, k2tog, k2, skpo, k6 in B; k3 in A; k7, k2tog, k1 in B. *(32 sts)*
Row 48: P1, p2tog, p7 in B; p1 in A; in B, p6, p2togtbl, p2, p2tog, p6, p2togtbl, p1 in B. *(28 sts)*
Break A and the strand of B currently at the center of the piece and use other strand of B.
Row 49: K1, skpo, k4, k2tog, k2, skpo, k12, k2tog, k1. *(24 sts)*
Row 50: P1, p2tog, p10, p2togtbl, p2, p2tog, p2, p2togtbl, p1. *(20 sts)*
Row 51: K1, skpo, k2tog, k2, skpo, k8, k2tog, k1. *(16 sts)*
Row 52: P1, p2tog, p6, p2tog, p2togtbl, p2tog, p1. *(12 sts)*
Break yarn, thread it through rem sts, and pull up securely.
Work thumb as for right mitten.

Ear
Make 4
Using US 3 (3.25mm) needles, cast on 6 sts in A.
Beg with a k row, work 2 rows in st st.
Row 3: Ssk, k2, k2tog. *(4 sts)*
Row 4: Purl.
Row 5: Ssk, k2tog. *(2 sts)*
Row 6: P2tog. *(1 st)*
Row 7: Inc. *(2 sts)*
Row 8: Purl.
Row 9: [Inc] twice. *(4 sts)*
Row 10: Purl.
Row 11: [Inc, k1] twice. *(6 sts)*
Beg with a p row, work 2 rows in st st.
Bind (cast) off kwise.

To make up
Join the side seams of the mittens and the thumb seams using flat stitch (see page 125).
Fold an ear piece in half lengthwise, right sides together, and sew the two sides, leaving the lower edge open. Turn the ear the right way out and oversew (see page 125) the lower edge. Make the other three ears in the same way and oversew in place.
Work French knots (see page 124) in black yarn for the eye centers, winding the yarn three times around the needle instead of the usual two. Using off-white yarn, work a circle of chain stitch (see page 124) around the eye center. For the nose, work a small coil of chain stitch using black yarn.
Weave in all loose ends.

marmalade kitten scarf

Kittens are one of the cutest baby animals: I happen to think marmalade kittens are the sweetest of the lot, so I knitted this scarf in two complementary shades of orange. But the scarf would look just as beautiful in shades of gray, or even plain black or white. So if you know someone who loves cats, why not knit them this scarf in a shade to match their own pet moggy? I can guarantee that it will be appreciated.

Yarn
Patons Merino Extrafine DK (100% wool) light worsted (DK) yarn
1 x 1¾oz (50g) ball (131yd/120m) in shade 00125 Orange (A)
1 x 1¾oz (50g) ball (131yd/120m) in shade 00123 Apricot (B)
Small amounts of black, off-white, and beige light worsted (DK) yarn

Needles and equipment
US 6 (4mm) knitting needles
Yarn sewing needle
Large-eyed embroidery needle

Gauge (tension)
22 sts and 30 rows in stockinette (stocking) stitch to a 4-in (10-cm) square on US 6 (4mm) needles.

Measurements
The finished scarf is 39¾in (101cm) long, including the back legs.

Abbreviations
See page 126.

To make scarf
Cast on 14 sts in A.
Row 1: Inc, k to last 2 sts, inc, k1. *(16 sts)*
Row 2: Purl.
Row 3: K1, m1, k to last st, m1, k1. *(18 sts)*
Row 4: Purl.
Rep rows 3–4, 5 times more. *(28 sts)*
Beg with a k row, work 17 rows in st st.
Leave A at side of work and join in B.
Row 32: Knit.
Row 33: K2, p to last 2 sts, k2.
Leave B at side of work and use A.
Row 34: Knit.
Row 35: K2, p to last 2 sts, k2.
Rep rows 32–35 (last 4 rows), 53 times more.

Break A and cont in B.

Knit 6 rows.

Shape back legs

Row 254: K6, bind (cast) off 16 sts, k to end.

Cont on 6 sts just knitted only, leaving rem sts on needle.

Knit 23 rows.

Shape paw

Next row: K2, turn and work on 2 sts just worked only.

*Knit 3 rows.

Next row: K2togtbl, [pick up and k 1 st down row ends, bind (cast) off 1 st] 3 times, k next st on needle, bind (cast) off 1 st, k1. *(2 sts)***

Rep from * to ** once more.

Knit 3 rows.

Next row: K2togtbl, [pick up and k 1 st down row ends, bind (cast) off 1 st] twice.

Break thread and pull rem st through.

Rejoin B to rem 9 sts on WS of work.

Knit 23 rows.

Shape paw as for first back leg.

Face

Cast on 14 sts in A.

Row 1: Inc, k to last 2 sts, inc, k1. *(16 sts)*

Row 2: Purl.

Leave A at side of work and join in B.

Row 3: K1, m1, k to last st, m1, k1. *(18 sts)*

Row 4: Purl.

Leave B at side of work and use A.

Row 5: K1, m1, k to last st, m1, k1. *(20 sts)*

Row 6: Purl.

Rep rows 3–6 (last 4 rows) twice more. *(28 sts)*

Leave A at side of work and use B.

Row 15: Knit.

Row 16: Purl.

Leave B at side of work and use A.

Row 17: Knit.

Row 18: Purl.

Rep rows 15–18 (last 4 rows), 3 times more.

Bind (cast) off.

Front leg

Make 2

Cast on 6 sts in B.

Knit 46 rows.

Shape paw as for back legs.

Ear

Make 2

Cast on 8 sts in A.

Beg with a k row, work 2 rows in st st.

Row 3: Skpo, k4, k2tog. *(6 sts)*

Row 4: Purl.

Row 5: Skpo, k2, k2tog. *(4 sts)*

Row 6: Purl.

Row 7: Skpo, k2tog. *(2 sts)*

Row 8: P2tog. *(1 st)*

Row 9: Inc. *(2 sts)*

Row 10: Purl.

Row 11: [Inc] twice. *(4 sts)*

Row 12: Purl.

Row 13: K1, m1, k2, m1, k1. *(6 sts)*

Row 14: Purl.

Row 15: K1, m1, k4, m1, k1. *(8 sts)*

Row 16: Purl.

Row 17: Knit.

Bind (cast) off.

Tail

Cast on 9 sts in A.

Beg with a k row, work 2 rows in st st.

Leave A at side of work and join in B.

Beg with a k row, work 2 rows in st st.

Rep last 4 rows in two-row stripe patt as set, 16 times more.

Break B and work remander of tail in A.

Beg with a k row, work 2 rows in st st.

Next row: Ssk, k5, k2tog. *(7 sts)*

Next row: Purl.

Break yarn, thread it through rem sts, and pull up securely.

To make up

For face, using black yarn, embroider two small circles using chain stitch (see page 124) for the centers of the eyes. Work a row of chain stitch around these circles using off-white yarn. Using black yarn, work a triangle shape in chain stitch for the nose, and work a line of chain stitch from the base of the nose to the lower edge of the face. Separate a length of beige light worsted (DK) yarn into two thinner strands and use them to embroider the whiskers in backstitch.

Place the face on the head part of the main scarf so that the right sides are together. Oversew the side seams (see page 125). Turn the head the right way out and sew the top edge in place using mattress stitch (see page 125). Oversew the front legs in place underneath the head, where the head meets the main part of the scarf.

Fold the ears so that the right side of the front and back pieces are together and oversew the two sides. Turn the right way out and sew the lower edge together using flat stitch (see page 125). Oversew the ears in place using the photograph as a guide.

Sew the back seam of the tail using flat stitch. Oversew the tail in place in the center of the kitten's lower end, just where the garter stitch border meets the main part of the scarf.

Weave in all loose ends.

CHAPTER 3
water lovers

Who doesn't love a water-loving beast? There are irresistible baby seals—immortalized in our big-eyed seal pup scarf—and there are snarly sharks—or actually in this case, a friendly, fuzzy one. And if they don't float your boat, try out your waddle in a pair of quirky knitted penguin socks.

tropical frog scarf

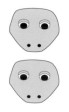

Not everyone loves the typical frog, which can be a little jumpy, a little slithery, and a little boring when it comes to color (sorry all you frog-lovers out there). But how can anyone resist all the beautiful colors of tropical frogs? Copy the colors of a real species, or just make up your own, as I have. If you don't fancy knitting the hooded eyes, simply get a matching pair of big buttons—or you could even use a pair of eyes made for crafts and toy making.

Yarn and materials
Katia Maxi Merino (55% merino, 45% acrylic) bulky (chunky) yarn.
2 x 3½oz (100g) balls (71yd/125m) in shade 018 (A)
1 x 3½oz (100g) ball (71yd/125m) in shade 033 (B)
Small amount of off-white light worsted (DK) yarn (C)
Small amount of black light worsted (DK) yarn
A handful of 100% polyester toy filling

Needles and equipment
US 9 (5.5mm) knitting needles
Yarn sewing needle
Large-eyed embroidery needle

Gauge (tension)
13 sts and 18 rows in stockinette (stocking) stitch to a 4-in (10-cm) square on US 9 (5.5mm) needles.

Measurements
The finished scarf is 51in (130cm) long.

Abbreviations
See page 126.

To make scarf
Cast on 10 sts in A.
Row 1: Inc, k to last st, inc, k1. *(12 sts)*
Row 2: Purl.
Row 3: K1, m1, k to last st, m1, k1. *(14 sts)*
Row 4: Purl.
Rep rows 3–4, 5 times more. *(24 sts)*
Beg with a k row, work 8 rows in st st.
Row 23: K2, ssk, k to last 4 sts, k2tog, k2. *(22 sts)*
Row 24: Purl.
Row 25: K2, ssk, k to last 4 sts, k2tog, k2. *(20 sts)*
Row 26: Knit.
Row 27: K3, p to last 3 sts, k3.
Rep rows 26–27 twice more.
Leave A at side (weaving it up first stitch of each k row until needed again) and join in B.
Row 32: Knit.
Row 33: K3, p to last 3 sts, k3.
Leave B at side (weaving it up first stitch of each k row until needed again) and use A.
Rep rows 26–33 (last 8 rows), 20 times more.
Break B and work remainder of scarf in A.
Row 194: Knit.
Row 195: K3, p to last 3 sts, k3.
Rep rows 194–195 twice more.
Knit 6 rows.
Shape back legs
Row 206: K7, bind (cast) off 6 sts, k to end.
Work on last group of 7 sts just worked, leaving rem sts on needle.
*Knit 11 rows.
Beg with a k row, work 22 rows in st st.
Shape foot
Next row: K2, turn and work on these 2 sts only, leaving rem sts on needle.
Beg with a p row, work 5 rows in st st.

Beg with a k row, work 8 rows in st st.
Row 23: K2, ssk, k to last 4 sts, k2tog, k2. *(22 sts)*
Row 24: Purl.
Row 25: K2, ssk, k to last 4 sts, k2tog, k2. *(20 sts)*
Row 26: Purl.
Bind (cast) off.

Eye hoods
Make 2
Cast on 3 sts in A.
Row 1: [Inc] 3 times. *(6 sts)*
Row 2: Knit.
Row 3: K1, [m1, k1] to end. *(11 sts)*
Row 4: Knit.
Bind (cast) off.

Eyeballs
Make 2
Cast on 4 sts using C double.
Row 1: [Inc] 4 times. *(8 sts)*
Row 2: Purl.
Row 3: K1, [m1, k1] to end. *(15 sts)*
Row 4: Purl.
Row 5: [K2tog] 3 times, sl1, k2tog, psso, [ssk] 3 times. *(7 sts)*
Break yarn, thread it through rem sts, and pull up securely.

To make up
Sew the eye hoods in place on the face so that the bound-(cast-) off edges form the outer rim of the eye hood. Join the side seam of the eyeballs using flat stitch (see page 125), stuffing lightly as you go. Place the eyeballs in the eye hoods. Stitch in place along the part of the eyeball that meets the main scarf and along the outer rim of the eye hood. Using black yarn, work the center of the eye in chain stitch (see page 124). Work two small circles of chain stitch in black yarn for the nostrils.
Place the face on the head part of the main scarf so that the right sides are together. Oversew (see page 125) the side seams. Turn the head the right way out and sew the top edge in place using mattress stitch (see page 125).
Oversew the front legs in place underneath the head, where the head meets the main part of the scarf.
Weave in all loose ends.

Next row: K2tog, [pick up and k 1 st from row ends, bind/cast off 1 st] 4 times (1 st rem on needle), k1, bind (cast) off 1 st, k2. Turn and work on these 3 sts only, leaving rem sts on needle.
Beg with a p row, work 5 rows in st st.
Next row: Sl1, k2tog, psso, [pick up and k 1 st from row ends, bind/cast off 1 st] 4 times (1 st rem on needle), k1, bind (cast) off 1 st, k1. Turn and work on these 2 sts only, leaving rem sts on needle.
Beg with a p row, work 5 rows in st st.
Next row: K2tog, [pick up and k 1 st from row ends, bind/cast off 1 st] 4 times. (1 st rem on needle.)
Break yarn and fasten off.
Rejoin A to second group of sts on needle on WS of work and rep from * to end.

Front leg
Make 2
Cast on 7 sts in A.
Beg with a k row, work 42 rows in st st.
Shape foot as for back legs.

Face
Cast on 10 sts in A.
Row 1: Inc, k to last st, inc, k1. *(12 sts)*
Row 2: Purl.
Row 3: K1, m1, k to last st, m1, k1. *(14 sts)*
Row 4: Purl.
Rep rows 3–4, 5 times more. *(24 sts)*

fish mittens

Knitted in a combination of beautifully soft yarns, these mittens are destined to delight young fish and fishing fans everywhere—and, in fact, just about anyone who doesn't like their accessories too plain. I've chosen a combination of bright pink and the gentlest of almond greens, but these mittens are the perfect opportunity to let your imagination go wild. Purple and yellow? Or turquoise and coral?

Yarn and materials

Sublime Natural Aran (100% wool) worsted (Aran) yarn
1 x 1¾oz (50g) ball (109yd/100m) in shade 423 Dilly (A)
Debbie Bliss Cashmerino Aran (55% wool, 33% acrylic, 12% cashmere) worsted (Aran) yarn
1 x 1¾oz (50g) ball (99yd/90m) in shade 076 Willow (B)
Small amounts of black and off-white light worsted (DK) yarn

Needles and equipment

US 8 (5mm) knitting needles
Yarn sewing needle
Large-eyed embroidery needle

Gauge (tension)

18 sts and 24 rows in stockinette (stocking) stitch to a 4-in (10-cm) square on US 8 (5mm) needles (both yarns).

Measurements

The finished mittens measure 7½in (19cm) from the base of the wrist to the tip and should fit an average size child of 7–10 years.

Abbreviations

See page 126.

Left mitten

Cast on 34 sts in A.
Row 1: [K1, p1] to end.
Rep row 1, 7 times more.
Break A and join in B.
Beg with a k row, work 4 rows in st st.
Row 13: K14, inc, k1, inc, k to end. *(36 sts)*
Row 14: Purl.
Row 15: K14, inc, k3, inc, k to end. *(38 sts)*
Row 16: Purl.
Row 17: K14, inc, k5, inc, k to end. *(40 sts)*
Row 18: Purl.
Row 19: K14, inc, k7, inc, k to end. *(42 sts)*
Beg with a p row, work 3 rows in st st.

Row 16: Purl.
Row 17: K17, inc, k5, inc, k to end. *(40 sts)*
Row 18: Purl.
Row 19: K17, inc, k7, inc, k to end. *(42 sts)*
Beg with a p row, work 3 rows in st st.
Shape thumb
Next row: K18 in B, leave B at side of work and join in A.
K10, turn and cast on 1 st.
Work remainder of right mitten as for left mitten from
* to end.

Fins
Make 4
Cast on 14 sts in A.
Row 1: K2togtbl, k to last 2 sts, k2togtbl. *(12 sts)*
Rep row 1, 4 times more. *(4 sts)*
Row 6: [K2togtbl] twice.
Row 7: K2tog. *(1 st)*
Break yarn and fasten off.

To make up
Join the side seams of the mittens using flat stitch (see page 125).
Place two of the fin pieces together and oversew (see page 125) around the edges, close to the edge, leaving the lower (cast-on) edge open. Turn the right way out. Make the second fin in the same way. Oversew the fins in place on the top of the mittens, using the photograph as a guide.
Using black yarn, work two French knots (see page 124) for the centers of the eyes. Using off-white yarn, work a circle of chain stitch (see page 124) around each of the French knots. Weave in all loose ends.

Shape thumb
Next row: K15 in B, leave B at side of work and join in A.
K10, turn and cast on 1 st.
***Next row:** P11, turn and cast on 1 st.
Work on these 12 sts just worked, leaving rem sts on needle.
Beg with a k row, work 6 rows in st st.
Next row: K1, [k2tog, k2] twice, k2tog, k1. *(9 sts)*
Next row: Purl.
Next row: [K1, k2tog] 3 times. *(6 sts)*
Break yarn, thread it through rem sts, and pull up securely.
With RS facing and using B, pick up and k 2 sts across base of thumb then k to end. *(34 sts)*
Beg with a p row, work 8 rows in st st.
Row 32: Knit.
Break B and work remainder of mitten in A.
Beg with a k row, work 6 rows in st st.
Row 39: K2, [skpo, k2] 4 times, [k2tog, k2] to end. *(26 sts)*
Beg with a p row, work 3 rows in st st.
Row 43: K2, [skpo] twice, k1, [k2tog] twice, k4, [skpo] twice, k1, [k2tog] twice, k2. *(18 sts)*
Row 44: Purl.
Row 45: K2, skpo, k1, k2tog, k4, skpo, k1, k2tog, k2. *(14 sts)*
Row 46: [P2tog] to end. *(7 sts)*
Break yarn, thread it through rem sts, and pull up securely.

Right mitten
Rows 1–12: Work as for left mitten.
Row 13: K17, inc, k1, inc, k to end. *(36 sts)*
Row 14: Purl.
Row 15: K17, inc, k3, inc, k to end. *(38 sts)*

here's a tip *Take your time when deciding on colors for your project. Choosing complementary colors usually works best. For some ideas, check out the "color wheels" that you can find online and in printed form.*

octopus scoodie

It's mainly a hat; I admit it. But those long legs are perfect for keeping your neck warm, so it's a bit of a cross between a scarf and a hat. And I've just learned that the name for this is a "scoodie." This octopus scoodie is knitted in a pastel seaside shade, in a soft chunky yarn that knits up a treat, and it would make a great first or second project for a newbie knitter.

Yarn and materials

Phildar Rapido (50% polyamide, 25% wool, 25% acrylic) bulky (chunky) yarn
3 x 1¾oz (50g) balls (45yd/41m) in shade 0018 Danube
Small amounts of black, off-white, and red light worsted (DK) yarn

Needles and equipment

US 10½ (6.5mm) knitting needles
2 stitch markers or small safety pins
Stitch holder
Yarn sewing needle
Large-eyed embroidery needle

Gauge (tension)

11 sts and 16 rows in stockinette (stocking) stitch to a 4-in (10-cm) square on US 10½ (6.5mm) needles.

Measurements

The hat part of the scoodie has a 16½in (42cm) circumference (unstretched) and should fit an average size child of 3–5 years.

Abbreviations

See page 126.

To make scoodie

Cast on 48 sts.
Mark 18th and 31st stitch with a stitch marker or small safety pin.
Knit 4 rows.
Beg with a k row, work 16 rows in st st.
Row 21: K3, [skpo, k6] 5 times, skpo, k3. *(42 sts)*
Row 22: Purl.
Row 23: K2, [sl2, k1, p2sso, k4] 5 times, sl2, k1, p2sso, k2. *(30 sts)*
Row 24: Purl.
Row 25: K1, [sl2, k1, p2sso, k2] 5 times, sl2, k1, p2sso, k1. *(18 sts)*
Row 26: [P2tog] 9 times.
Break yarn, thread it through rem sts, and pull up securely.
With RS facing, pick up and k 18 sts along cast-on edge from corner to first stitch marker.
Row 1: Ssk, k to end. *(17 sts)*
Row 2: Knit.
Rep rows 1–2 once more. *(16 sts)*
*Next row: K4, put rem sts on stitch holder and cont on 4 sts just knitted only.
Knit 75 rows.
Next row: Ssk, k2tog. *(2 sts)*
Next row: K2tog. *(1 st)*
Break yarn and fasten off.**
Put sts back on needle.
Rep from * to ** twice more.
Next row: Knit rem 4 sts.
Knit 75 rows.
Next row: Ssk, k2tog. *(2 sts)*
Next row: K2tog. *(1 st)*
Break yarn and fasten off.
With RS facing, pick up and k 18 sts along cast-on edge from second stitch marker to corner.
Row 1: Knit to last 2 sts, k2tog. *(17 sts)*
Row 2: Knit.
Rep rows 1–2 once more. *(16 sts)*

*Next row: K4, put rem sts on stitch holder and cont on 4 sts just knitted only.
Knit 75 rows.
Next row: Ssk, k2tog. *(2 sts)*
Next row: K2tog. *(1 st)*
Break yarn and fasten off.**
Put sts back on needle.
Rep from * to ** twice more.
Next row: Knit rem 4 sts.
Knit 75 rows.
Next row: Ssk, k2tog. *(2 sts)*
Next row: K2tog. *(1 st)*
Break yarn and fasten off.

To make up
Join the back seam of the scoodie using flat stitch (see page 125). Using black yarn, work a small coil of chain stitch (see page 124) for the centers of the eyes. Using off-white yarn, work a circle of chain stitch around each eye center. Using red yarn, work a curve of chain stitch for the mouth.
Weave in all loose ends.

shark scarf

Sharks are scary… fierce… cold… horrible… but not this one: this is certainly the most adorable shark you'll ever meet. I know there's something fascinating about these super-fish, but I didn't really like their awesome reputation, so I took the raw ingredients and came up with this lovely fellow. He's cool-looking and sleek, but warm and cozy, and utterly irresistible.

Yarn
Wendy Pampas Mega Chunky (70% acrylic, 30% wool) super-bulky (super-chunky) yarn
2 x 3½oz (100g) balls (62yd/57m) in shade 2244 Silver (A)
Small amounts of black, white, and gray light worsted (DK) yarn

Needles and equipment
US 15 (10mm) knitting needles
Yarn sewing needle
Large-eyed embroidery needle

Gauge (tension)
9 sts and 13 rows in stockinette (stocking) stitch to a 4-in (10-cm) square on US 15 (10mm) needles.

Measurements
The finished scarf is 41in (104cm) long.

Abbreviations
See page 126.

To make scarf
Cast on 2 sts in A.
Row 1: Inc, k1. *(3 sts)*
Row 2: Knit.
Row 3: [Inc] twice, k1. *(5 sts)*
Row 4: K2, p1, k2.
Row 5: K2, m1, k to last 2 sts, m1, k2. *(7 sts)*
Row 6: K2, p to last 2 sts, k2.
Row 7: Knit.
Row 8: K2, p to last 2 sts, k2.
Rep rows 5–8, 4 times more. *(15 sts)*
Row 25: Knit.
Row 26: K2, p to last 2 sts, k2.
Rep rows 25–26, 12 times more.
Row 51: Knit.
Row 52: P to last 2 sts, k2.
Rep rows 51–52, 7 times more.

Row 67: Knit.

Row 68: K2, p to last 2 sts, k2.

Rep rows 67–68, 7 times more.

Row 83: K2, ssk, k to last 4 sts, k2tog, k2. *(13 sts)*

Row 84: K2, p to last 2 sts, k2.

Row 85: Knit.

Row 86: K2, p to last 2 sts, k2.

Rep rows 85–86, 4 times more.

Rep rows 83–94 (last 12 rows) once more.

Row 107: K2, ssk, k to last 4 sts, k2tog, k2. *(11 sts)*

Row 108: K2, p to last 2 sts, k2.

Row 109: Knit.

Row 110: K2, p to last 2 sts, k2.

Rep rows 109–110 twice more.

Shape tail

Row 115: K2, m1, k to last 2 sts, m1, k2. *(13 sts)*

Row 116: K2, p to last 2 sts, k2.

Rep rows 115–116 twice more. *(17 sts)*

Row 121: K2, m1, k6, turn and cont on 9 sts just worked, leaving rem sts on needle.

Next row: K2, p to last 2 sts, k2.

Next row: Knit to last 4 sts, k2tog, k2. *(8 sts)*

Next row: K2, p to last 2 sts, k2.

Rep last 2 rows, 3 times more. *(5 sts)*

Next row: K1, k2tog, k2. *(4 sts)*

Next row: Knit.

Next row: K2tog, k2. *(3 sts)*

Next row: Sl1, k2tog, psso. *(1 st)*

Break yarn and fasten off.

Rejoin yarn to rem 9 sts on RS of work.

Next row: Knit to last 2 sts, m1, k2. *(10 sts)*

Next row: K2, p to last 2 sts, k2.

Next row: K2, skpo, k to end. *(9 sts)*

Next row: K2, p to last 2 sts, k2.

Rep last 2 rows, 4 times more. *(5 sts)*

Next row: K2, skpo, k1. *(4 sts)*

Next row: Knit.

Next row: K2, skpo. *(3 sts)*

Next row: Sl1, skpo, pass first slipped stitch over.

Break yarn and fasten off.

Dorsal fin

The dorsal fin is knitted onto the part of the edge without the garter stitch border. With RS facing, pick up and k 15 sts across center edge of scarf, beg on 2nd ridge of garter stitch border to one side of plain edge and ending on 2nd ridge of garter stitch border on the other side.

Row 1 (WS): K1, p to last st, k1.

Row 2: K1, m1, k to last 3 sts, skpo, k1.

Row 3: K1, p2tog, p to last st, k1. *(14 sts)*

Rep rows 2–3, 3 times more. *(11 sts)*

Row 10: Knit to last 3 sts, skpo, k1. *(10 sts)*

Row 11: K1, p2tog, p to last st, k1. *(9 sts)*

Rep rows 10–11 twice more. *(5 sts)*

Row 16: K2tog, k1, skpo. *(3 sts)*

Row 17: Sl1, k2tog, psso. *(1 st)*

Break yarn and fasten off.

To make up

Using black yarn, embroider a small coil of chain stitch (see page 124) for the eye and a line of chain stitch for the mouth. Using white yarn, embroider some lazy daisy stitches (see page 124) for the teeth. Using gray yarn, work three arcs of chain stitch for the gills.

Weave in all loose ends.

alligator scarf

If you're in the market for a safe, trouble-free reptile—one that's cute rather than scary—then here is the scarf you've been waiting for. I've knitted this striking fellow in a lovely soft yarn in a mid-green shade. He's worked in a textured stitch that is extremely simple once you get into the swing of it. And because the yarn is chunky, you'll find that he grows pretty quickly. I've given this alligator knitted eyes and nostrils, but if you want something super simple, you could always use some big buttons instead.

Yarn
Wendy Serenity Chunky (70% acrylic, 20% alpaca, 10% wool) bulky (chunky) yarn
2 x 3½oz (100g) balls (87yd/80m) in shade 3202 Ivy (A)
Small amount of light worsted (DK) yarn in off-white (B)
Small amount of black light worsted (DK) yarn
A handful of 100% polyester toy filling

Needles and equipment
US 10½ (6.5mm) knitting needles
Yarn sewing needle
Large-eyed embroidery needle

Gauge (tension)
14 sts and 20 rows in stockinette (stocking) stitch to a 4-in (10-cm) square on US 10½ (6.5mm) needles in main yarn (A)

Measurements
The finished scarf is 64½in (164cm) long.

Abbreviations
See page 126.

To make scarf
Cast on 2 sts in A.
Row 1: [Inc] twice. *(4 sts)*
Row 2: Knit.
Row 3: [Inc, k1] twice. *(6 sts)*
Row 4: Knit.
Row 5: Inc, k3, inc, k1. *(8 sts)*
Knit 11 rows.
Row 17: K2, m1, k to last 2 sts, m1, k2. *(10 sts)*
Knit 9 rows.
Rep rows 17–26 (last 10 rows) 3 times more. *(16 sts)*
Row 57: K4, p2, [k1, p2] to last 4 sts, k4.
Row 58: K3, [p1, k2] to last 4 sts, p1, k3.
Row 59: Knit.
Row 60: K3, p to last 3 sts, k3.
Rep rows 57–60 once more.
Row 65: K3, m1, [k1, p2] to last 4 sts, k1, m1, k3. *(18 sts)*
Row 66: K4, [p1, k2] to last 5 sts, p1, k4.
Row 67: Knit.
Row 68: K3, p to last 3 sts, k3.
Row 69: K3, p1, [k1, p2] to last 5 sts, k1, p1, k3.
Row 70: K4, [p1, k2] to last 5 sts, p1, k4.
Row 71: Knit.
Row 72: K3, p to last 3 sts, k3.
Row 73: K3, m1, p1, [k1, p2] to last 5 sts, k1, p1, m1, k3. *(20 sts)*
Row 74: K5, [p1, k2] to last 6 sts, p1, k5.
Row 75: Knit.
Row 76: K3, p to last 3 sts, k3.
Row 77: K3, p2, [k1, p2] to last 3 sts, k3.
Row 78: K5, [p1, k2] to last 3 sts, k3.
Row 79: Knit.
Row 80: K3, p to last 3 sts, k3.
Row 81: K3, m1, p2, [k1, p2] to last 3 sts, m1, k3. *(22 sts)*
Row 82: K3, [p1, k2] to last 4 sts, p1, k3.
Row 83: Knit.
Row 84: K3, p to last 3 sts, k3.

Eyeballs

Make 2

Cast on 4 sts using B double.

Row 1: [Inc] 4 times.
Row 2: Purl.
Row 3: K1, [m1, k1] to end. *(15 sts)*
Row 4: Purl.
Row 5: [K2tog] 3 times, sl1, k2tog, psso, [ssk] 3 times. *(7 sts)*
Break yarn, thread it through rem sts, and pull up securely.

Nostrils

Make 2

Cast on 2 sts in A.

Row 1: [Inc] twice. *(4 sts)*
Row 2: Knit.
Row 3: K1, [m1, k1] to end. *(7 sts)*
Row 4: Knit.
Bind (cast) off.

To make up

Sew the eye hoods in place so that the bound- (cast-) off edges form the outer rim of the eye hood. Join the side seam of the eyeballs using flat stitch (see page 125), stuffing lightly as you go. Place the eyeballs in the eye hoods. Stitch in place along the part of the eyeball that meets the main scarf and along the outer rim of the eye hood. Stitch the nostrils in place so that the bound- (cast-) off edge forms the outer rim of the nostril. Using black yarn, work the center of the eye in chain stitch (see page 124).

Weave in all loose ends.

Row 85: K4, p2, [k1, p2] to last 4 sts, k4.
Row 86: K3, [p1, k2] to last 4 sts, p1, k3.
Row 87: Knit.
Row 88: K3, p to last 3 sts, k3.
Rep rows 65–88 once more. *(28 sts)*
Rep rows 85–88 (last 4 rows), 32 times more.
Rep rows 85–86 once more.
Knit 16 rows.
Row 259: K3, ssk, k to last 5 sts, k2tog, k3. *(26 sts)*
Knit 5 rows.
Rep rows 259–264 (last 6 rows) twice more. *(22 sts)*
Row 277: K3, ssk, k to last 5 sts, k2tog, k3. *(20 sts)*
Knit 3 rows.
Rep rows 277–280 (last 4 rows) once more. *(18 sts)*
Knit 8 rows.
Row 293: K3, m1, k to last 3 sts, m1, k3. *(20 sts)*
Knit 3 rows.
Rep rows 293–296 (last 4 rows) once more. *(22 sts)*
Row 301: K3, ssk, k to last 5 sts, k2tog, k2. *(20 sts)*
Row 302: Ssk, k to last 2 sts, k2tog. *(18 sts)*
Rep rows 301–302 once more. *(14 sts)*
Bind (cast) off.

Eye hoods

Make 2

Cast on 3 sts in A.

Row 1: [Inc] 3 times. *(6 sts)*
Row 2: Knit.
Row 3: K1, [m1, k1] to end. *(11 sts)*
Row 4: Knit.
Bind (cast) off.

---

here's a tip *If you need just a small amount of a yarn to embroider a project, check out the supplies in thrift stores, buy small balls of yarn aimed at toy makers, or buy a small skein of tapestry yarn.*

frog socks

Can anything be much more fun than leaping about in a pair of your very own frog socks? Well, I don't think so. And if you don't fancy jumping about, you can always just wiggle your toes and let your sock-frogs croak to each other. I love the two-tone green look for these socks, but if you prefer, you can knit your own tropical frog version. Who am I to dictate your look?

Yarn
Sublime Extrafine Merino Wool DK (100% wool) light worsted (DK) yarn
1 x 1¾oz (50g) ball (127yd/116m) in shade 0019 Waterleaf (A)
Patons Merino Extrafine DK (100% wool) light worsted (DK) yarn
1 x 1¾oz (50g) ball (131yd/120m) in shade 00173 Apple Green (B)
Small amount of light worsted (DK) yarn in off-white (C)
Small amounts of black and red light worsted (DK) yarn
A small handful of 100% polyester toy filling

Needles and equipment
US 8 (5mm) knitting needles
A set of 4 (or 5) US 6 (4mm) double-pointed needles (DPNs) or a US 6 (4mm) short circular needle designed for knitting socks and other smaller items (see page 122 for more information on knitting on DPNs and circular needles)
US 5 (3.75mm) knitting needles
Stitch marker or small safety pin
Yarn sewing needle
Large-eyed embroidery needle

Gauge (tension)
22 sts and 30 rows in stockinette (stocking) stich to a 4-in (10-cm) square on US 6 (4mm) needles in B.

Measurements
The finished socks measure 7in (18 cm) from the heel to the tip of the toe. They should fit a child's shoe size US 11½ –12½ (UK 10½–11½/EU 29 –30)

Abbreviations
See page 126.

To make socks
Make 2
Using US 8 (5mm) needles, cast on 40 sts in A. Transfer sts to DPNs or circular needle and mark your first cast-on stitch with stitch marker or small safety pin.
Round 1: [K2, p2] to end.
Rep round 1, 6 times more.
Break A and join in B.
Knit 22 rounds.
Shape heel back
Break B and join in A.
Row 1: K10, turn. *(10 sts)*
Row 2: P20. *(20 sts)*
(If using DPNs, keep all 20 sts on one needle.)
Row 3: Sl1, k1 to end.
Row 4: Sl1 pwise, p to end.
Rep rows 3–4, 9 times more.

Shape heel base
Row 23: K12, ssk, k1, turn. *(19 sts)*
Row 24: Sl1 pwise, p5, p2tog, p1, turn. *(18 sts)*
Row 25: Sl1, k6, ssk, k1, turn. *(17 sts)*
Row 26: Sl1 pwise, p7, p2tog, p1, turn. *(16 sts)*
Row 27: Sl1, k8, ssk, k1, turn. *(15 sts)*
Row 28: Sl1 pwise, p9, p2tog, p1, turn. *(14 sts)*
Row 29: Sl1, k10, ssk, turn. *(13 sts)*
Row 30: Sl1, p10, p2tog, turn. *(12 sts)*
Shape foot
Break A and join in B and work remainder of sock in B.
Row 31 and forming base for rounds: Knit, putting stitch marker or safety pin between 6th and 7th sts to mark back of sock. With empty needle if using DPNs, pick up and k 10 sts up first side of heel back then k across 20 sts of top part of sock.
With another empty needle if using DPNs, pick up and k 10 sts down side of second heel back and then k 6 sts along base of heel (to stitch marker). These 52 sts will form the foot part of the sock.
Round 1: K13, k2tog, k22, ssk, k13. *(50 sts)*
Round 2: Knit.
Round 3: K12, k2tog, k22, ssk, k12. *(48 sts)*
Round 4: Knit.
Round 5: K11, k2tog, k22, ssk, k11. *(46 sts)*
Round 6: Knit.
Round 7: K10, k2tog, k22, ssk, k10. *(44 sts)*
Round 8: Knit.
Round 9: K9, k2tog, k22, ssk, k9. *(42 sts)*

Round 10: Knit.
Round 11: K8, k2tog, k22, ssk, k8. *(40 sts)*
Knit 23 more rounds.
Shape toe
Round 1: K7, ssk, k2, k2tog, k14, ssk, k2, k2tog, k7. *(36 sts)*
Round 2: Knit.
Round 1: K6, ssk, k2, k2tog, k12, ssk, k2, k2tog, k6. *(32 sts)*
Round 2: Knit.
Round 3: K5, ssk, k2, k2tog, k10, ssk, k2, k2tog, k5. *(28 sts)*
Round 4: Knit.
Round 5: K4, ssk, k2, k2tog, k8, ssk, k2, k2tog, k4. *(24 sts)*
Round 6: Knit.
Round 7: K3, ssk, k2, k2tog, k6, ssk, k2, k2tog, k3. *(20 sts)*
Round 8: K2, ssk, k2, k2tog, k4, ssk, k2, k2tog, k2. *(16 sts)*
Round 9: K1, ssk, k2, k2tog, k2, ssk, k2, k2tog, k1. *(12 sts)*
Break yarn, thread it through rem sts, and pull up securely.

Eye hoods
Make 4
Using US 5 (3.75mm) needles, cast on 3 sts in B.
Row 1: [Inc] 3 times. *(6 sts)*
Row 2: Knit.
Row 3: K1, [m1, k1] to end. *(11 sts)*
Row 4: Knit.
Bind (cast) off.

Eyeballs
Make 4
Using US 5 (3.75mm) needles, cast on 3 sts in C.
Row 1: [Inc] 3 times. *(6 sts)*
Row 2: Purl.
Row 3: [Inc] 6 times. *(12 sts)*
Row 4: Purl.
Row 5: [K2tog] to end. *(6 sts)*
Row 6: [P2tog] to end. *(3 sts)*
Break yarn, thread it through rem sts, and pull up securely.

To make up
Sew the eye hoods in place so that the bound- (cast-) off edges form the outer rim of the eye hood. Join the side seam of the eyeballs using flat stitch (see page 125), stuffing lightly as you go. Place the eyeballs in the eye hoods. Stitch in place along the part of the eyeball that meets the main part of the sock and along the outer rim of the eye hood. Using black yarn, work a small circle of chain stitch (see page 124) for the eye centers. In black yarn, work two straight stitches (see page 124) for the nostrils. In red yarn, work a row of chain stitch for the mouth along the toe end of the sock.
Weave in all loose ends.

fish scarf

If you're lucky enough to be walking along the coast—or even messing about on the river—a fish scarf has got to be the perfect accessory. I've knitted this one in marine-like shades of soft green and turquoise, and love the color-block look of the two colors together. But I admit that this fish isn't based on a real-life species, so please feel free to knit your fish in whatever shades you fancy.

Yarn

Sirdar Country Style DK (40% nylon, 30% wool, 30% acrylic) light worsted (DK) yarn
1 x 1¾oz (50g) ball (170yd/155m) in shade 0390 Tana (A)
Wendy Serenity Chunky (20% Alpaca, 70% acrylic, 10% wool) bulky (chunky) yarn
2 x 3½oz (100g) balls (87yd/80m) in shade 3208 Tourmaline (B)
Small amounts of black, off-white, and red light worsted (DK) yarn

Needles and equipment

US 10½ (6.5mm) knitting needles
Yarn sewing needle
Large-eyed embroidery needle

Gauge (tension)

14 sts and 20 rows in stockinette (stocking) stitch to a 4-in (10-cm) square on US 10½ (6.5mm) needles using B.

Measurements

The finished scarf is 55½in (141cm) long.

Abbreviations

See page 126.

To make scarf

Cast on 35 sts using A double.
Row 1: [P3, k1] to last 3 sts, p3.
Row 2: [K3, p1] to last 3 sts, k3.
Row 3: [P3, k1] to last 3 sts, p3.
Row 4: K1, ssk, p1, [k3, p1] to last 3 sts, k2tog, k1. *(33 sts)*
Row 5: P2, k1, [p3, k1] to last 2 sts, p2.
Row 6: K2, p1, [k3, p1] to last 2 sts, k2.
Row 7: P2, k1, [p3, k1] to last 2 sts, p2.
Row 8: K2, p1, ssk, k1, p1, [k3, p1] to last 6 sts, k1, k2tog, p1, k2. *(31 sts)*
Row 9: [P2, k1] twice, [p3, k1] 5 times, p2, k1, p2.
Row 10: [K2, p1] twice, [k3, p1] 5 times, k2, p1, k2.
Row 11: [P2, k1] twice, [p3, k1] 5 times, p2, k1, p2.
Row 12: [K2, p1] twice, ssk, k1, p1, [k3, p1] 3 times, k1, k2tog, [p1, k2] twice. *(29 sts)*
Row 13: [P2, k1] 3 times, [p3, k1] 3 times, [p2, k1] twice, p2.
Row 14: [K2, p1] 3 times, [k3, p1] 3 times, [k2, p1] twice, k2.
Row 15: [P2, k1] 3 times, [p3, k1] 3 times, [p2, k1] twice, p2.
Row 16: [K2, p1] 3 times, ssk, k1, p1, k3, p1, k1, k2tog, [p1, k2] 3 times. *(27 sts)*
Row 17: [P2, k1] 4 times, p3, [k1, p2] 4 times.
Row 18: [K2, p1] 4 times, k3, [p1, k2] 4 times.
Rep rows 17–18, 4 times more.
Break A and join in B.
Row 27: Knit
Row 28: K2, [p3, k2] to end.
Row 29: P2, [sl1 pwise, k2, psso, p2] to end.
Row 30: K2, [p1, yo, p1, k2] to end.
Row 31: P2, [k3, p2] to end.
Row 32: K2, [p3, k2] to end.
Rep rows 29–32, 40 times.
Rep rows 29–31 once.
Break B and rejoin A, using yarn double.
Row 196: Knit.
Row 197: Knit.
Row 198: K2, p to last 2 sts, k2.
Rep rows 197–198, 3 times more.
Row 205: K1, ssk, k to last 3 sts, k2tog, k1. *(25 sts)*

Row 206: K2, p to last 2 sts, k2.
Rep rows 205–206, 5 times more. *(15 sts)*
Row 217: K2, [ssk] twice, k3, [k2tog] twice, k2. *(11 sts)*
Row 218: K2, p to last 2 sts, k2.
Row 219: K2, ssk, k3, k2tog, k2. *(9 sts)*
Row 220: P2tog, p5, p2togtbl. *(7 sts)*
Row 221: Ssk, k3, k2tog. *(5 sts)*
Row 222: P2tog, p1, p2togtbl. *(3 sts)*
Row 223: Sl1, k2tog, psso. *(1 st)*
Break yarn and fasten off.

To make up

Using black yarn, embroider a small coil of chain stitch (see page 124) for the center of the eye. Using off-white yarn, work two coils of chain stitch around the eye center. Using a separated strand of black yarn, work three straight stitches (see page 124) above the eye for the eye lashes. Work the mouth in chain stitch using red yarn.
Weave in all loose ends.

penguin socks

With these super-warm penguin socks, you'll almost be ready to join the penguins themselves, waddling on the Antarctic ice. Well, okay… perhaps not quite. But you'll certainly be ready to face the chilliest of winter evenings. The socks are knitted on double-pointed needles or a circular needle, and the white tummy panel means they're not quite as straightforward as the other sock patterns in this book. So if you're new to sock knitting, give one of the simpler sock patterns a go first. But if you've got a bit of experience under your belt, please give these a go: you won't be disappointed.

Yarn

Lion Brand Wool Ease (80% acrylic, 20% wool) worsted (Aran) yarn
1 x 3oz (85g) ball (197yd/180m) in shade 153 Black (A)
1 x 3oz (85g) ball (197yd/180m) in shade 099 Fisherman (B)
1 x 3oz (85g) ball (197yd/180m) in shade 171 Gold (C)

Needles and equipment

US 10 (6mm) knitting needles
A set of 4 (or 5) US 8 (5mm) double-pointed needles (DPNs) or a US 8 (5mm) short circular needle designed for knitting socks and other smaller items (see page 122 for more information on knitting on DPNs and circular needles)
US 6 (4mm) knitting needles
Stitch marker or small safety pin
Yarn sewing needle
Large-eyed embroidery needle

Gauge (tension)

18 sts and 24 rows in stockinette (stocking) stich to a 4-in (10-cm) square on US 8 (5mm) needles.

Measurements

The finished socks measure 8in (20cm) from the heel to the tip of the toe. They should fit an adult's shoe size US 7½-9½ (UK 5–7/EU 38–40)

Abbreviations

See page 126.

To make socks

Make 2

Using US 10 (6mm) needles, cast on 40 sts in A. Transfer sts to DPNs or circular needle and mark your first cast-on stitch with stitch marker or small safety pin.
Round 1: [K2, p2] to end.
Rep round 1, 8 times more.
Knit 16 rounds.
For the penguin's white front panel, you will need to work this part of the sock in rows, wrapping and turning at the end of each row to avoid the need for sewing seams.
Row 1: K19 in A; join in B and k2; k19 in A, using strand from center of ball, WT.
Row 2: P18 in A; p4 in B; p18 in A, WT.
Row 3: K17 in A; k6 in B; k17 in A, WT.
Row 4: P16 in A; p8 in B; p16 in A, WT.
Row 5: K15 in A; k10 in B; k15 in A, WT.
Row 6: P14 in A; p12 in B; p14 in A, WT.
Row 7: K13 in A; k14 in B; k13 in A, WT.
Row 8: P12 in A; p16 in B; p12 in A, WT.
Row 9: K12 in A; k16 in B; k12 in A, WT.
Row 10: P12 in A; p16 in B; p12 in A, WT.
Rep rows 9–10, 10 times more.
Break B and work till toe of sock in A only.
Shape heel back
Row 1: K10, turn. *(10 sts)*
Row 2: P20. *(20 sts)*
(If using DPNs, keep all 20 sts on one needle.)
Row 3: Sl1, k to end.
Row 4: Sl1 pwise, p to end.
Rep rows 3–4, 7 times more.
Shape heel base
Row 19: K12, ssk, k1, turn. *(19 sts)*
Row 20: Sl1 pwise, p5, p2tog, p1, turn. *(18 sts)*
Row 21: Sl1, k6, ssk, k1, turn. *(17 sts)*
Row 22: Sl1 pwise, p7, p2tog, p1, turn. *(16 sts)*

Shape toe

Round 1: K6, ssk, k2, k2tog, k12, ssk, k2, k2tog, k6. *(32 sts)*
Round 2: Knit.
Round 3: K5, ssk, k2, k2tog, k10, ssk, k2, k2tog, k5. *(28 sts)*
Round 4: Knit.
Round 5: K4, ssk, k2, k2tog, k8, ssk, k2, k2tog, k4. *(24 sts)*
Round 6: Knit.
Round 7: K3, ssk, k2, k2tog, k6, ssk, k2, k2tog, k3. *(20 sts)*
Round 8: Knit.
Round 9: K2, ssk, k2, k2tog, k4, ssk, k2, k2tog, k2. *(16 sts)*
Round 10: K1, ssk, k2, k2tog, k2, ssk, k2, k2tog, k1. *(12 sts)*
Break yarn, thread it through rem sts, and pull up securely.

Beak

Using US 6 (4mm) needles, cast on 8 sts in C.
Beg with a k row, work 2 rows in st st.
Row 3: K1, ssk, k2, k2tog, k1. *(6 sts)*
Row 4: Purl.
Row 5: K1, ssk, k2tog, k1. *(4 sts)*
Row 6: [P2tog] twice. *(2 sts)*
Row 7: K2tog. *(1 st)*
Break yarn, pull through rem st, and pull up securely.

To make up

For the eyes, work a small circle of chain stitch (see page 124) in B. Using A, work a large French knot (see page 124) in the middle of the circle.
Fold the beak piece in half lengthwise and oversew (see page 125) the seam. With the seam facing downward, oversew the beak in place on the front of the socks, just above the top of the white front panel.
Weave in all loose ends.

Row 23: Sl1, k8, ssk, k1, turn. *(15 sts)*
Row 24: Sl1 pwise, p9, p2tog, p1, turn. *(14 sts)*
Row 25: Sl1, k10, ssk, turn. *(13 sts)*
Row 26: Sl1, p10, p2tog, turn. *(12 sts)*
Shape foot
Row 27 and forming base for rounds: Knit, putting stitch marker or safety pin between 6th and 7th sts to mark back of sock. With empty needle if using DPNs, pick up and k 10 sts up first side of heel back then k across 20 sts of top part of sock.
With another empty needle if using DPNs, pick up and k 10 sts down side of second heel back and then k 6 sts along base of heel (to stitch marker). These 52 sts will form the foot part of the sock.
Round 1: K13, k2tog, k22, ssk, k13. *(50 sts)*
Round 2: Knit.
Round 3: K12, k2tog, k22, ssk, k12. *(48 sts)*
Round 4: Knit.
Round 5: K11, k2tog, k22, ssk, k11. *(46 sts)*
Round 6: Knit.
Round 7: K10, k2tog, k22, ssk, k10. *(44 sts)*
Round 8: Knit.
Round 9: K9, k2tog, k22, ssk, k9. *(42 sts)*
Round 10: Knit.
Round 11: K8, k2tog, k22, ssk, k8. *(40 sts)*
Round 12: Knit.
Round 13: K7, k2tog, k22, ssk, k7. *(38 sts)*
Round 14: Knit.
Round 15: K6, k2tog, k22, ssk, k6. *(36 sts)*
Knit 13 more rounds.
Break B and join in C.

here's a tip

When you are changing colors of yarn in a single row (see page 121), don't pull the yarn up too tightly or your work looks puckered. It's always a good idea to practice the technique on a sample swatch first.

seal pup scarf

With their big eyes and fluffy white coats, baby seals have definitely got the "aah" factor. So capture a bit of that for yourself by knitting this gorgeous baby seal scarf. The combination of yarns, which includes mohair as well as alpaca, is simply stunning. And to make things even better, the seal scarf is one of the easiest in the book to make and an ideal second or third project for new knitters.

Yarn
Wendy Serenity Chunky (20% alpaca, 70% acrylic, 10% wool) bulky (chunky) yarn
2 x 3½oz (100g) balls (87yd/80m) in shade 3213 Cream (A)
Wendy Air (70% kid mohair, 30% nylon) lace weight yarn
1 x ¾oz (25g) ball (219yd/200m) in shade 2612 Lottie (B)
Small amount of black light worsted (DK) yarn

Needles and equipment
US 10½ (6.5mm) knitting needles
4 stitch markers or small safety pins
Yarn sewing needle
Large-eyed embroidery needle

Gauge (tension)
11 sts and 16 rows in stockinette (stocking) stitch to a 4-in (10-cm) square on US 10½ (6.5mm) needles using A and B held together.

Measurements
The finished scarf is 38in (97cm) long.

Abbreviations
See page 126.

To make scarf
Cast on 8 sts using A and B held together.
Row 1: Inc, k to last 2 sts, inc, k1. *(10 sts)*
Row 2: Knit.
Row 3: K2, m1, k to last 2 sts, m1, k2. *(12 sts)*
Row 4: K2, p to last 2 sts, k2.
Rep rows 3–4, 5 times more. *(22 sts)*
Row 15: Knit.
Place a stitch marker or small safety pin each end of the row just knitted.
Row 16: K2, p to last 2 sts, k2.
Row 17: Knit.
Row 18: K2, p to last 2 sts, k2.
Rep rows 17–18, 9 times more.
Place a stitch marker or small safety pin each end of the row just knitted.
Rep rows 17–18 twice more.
Row 41: K2, ssk, k to last 4 sts, k2tog, k2. *(20 sts)*
Row 42: K2, p to last 2 sts, k2.

Row 43: Knit.
Row 44: K2, p to last 2 sts, k2.
Rep rows 43–44, 36 times more.
Row 117: K2, ssk, k to last 4 sts, k2tog, k2. *(18 sts)*
Row 118: K2, p to last 2 sts, k2.
Row 119: Knit.
Row 120: K2, p to last 2 sts, k2.
Rep rows 119–120, 8 times more.
Row 137: K2, m1, k to last 2 sts, m1, k2. *(20 sts)*

Shape tail flippers
Row 138: K2, p6, k2, turn and work on these 10 sts only, leaving rem sts on needle.
Next row: Knit.
Next row: K2, p to last 2 sts, k2.
Next row: Knit to last 2 sts, m1, k2. *(11 sts)*
Next row: K2, p to last 2 sts, k2.
Next row: Knit.
Next row: K2, p to last 2 sts, k2.
Rep last 4 rows once more. *(12 sts)*
***Next row:** K2, ssk, k to last 4 sts, k2tog, k2. *(10 sts)*
Next row: K2, p to last 2 sts, k2.
Rep last 2 rows once more. *(8 sts)*
Next row: K2, ssk, k2tog, k2. *(6 sts)*
Next row: Ssk, k2, k2tog. *(4 sts)*
Next row: Ssk, k2tog. *(2 sts)*
Next row: K2tog. *(1 st)*
Break yarn and fasten off.
Rejoin yarn to rem 10 sts on WS of work.
Next row: K2, p to last 2 sts, k2.
Next row: Knit.
Next row: K2, p to last 2 sts, k2.

Next row: K2, m1, k to end. *(11 sts)*
Next row: K2, p to last 2 sts, k2.
Next row: Knit.
Next row: K2, p to last 2 sts, k2.
Rep last 4 rows once more. *(12 sts)***
Rep from * to **.

Flippers

With RS facing, pick up and k 14 sts on one edge between the marker nearest the face and the marker nearest the tail.
Row 2: K2, p to last 2 sts, k2.
Row 3: K2, k2tog, k to last 2 sts, m1, k2.
Row 4: K2, p to last 2 sts, k2.
Rep rows 2–3 twice more.
Row 9: K2, k2tog, k to end. *(13 sts)*
Row 10: K2, p to last 2 sts, k2.
Rep rows 9–10 once more. *(12 sts)*
***Row 13:** K2, ssk, k to last 4 sts, k2tog, k2. *(10 sts)*
Row 14: K2, p to last 2 sts, k2.
Row 15: K1, ssk, k to last 3 sts, k2tog, k1. *(8 sts)*
Row 16: K1, ssk, k2, k2tog, k1. *(6 sts)*
Row 17: Ssk, k2, k2tog. *(4 sts)*
Bind (cast) off.
With RS facing, pick up and k 14 sts on the other edge between the marker nearest the tail and the marker nearest the face.
Row 2: K2, p to last 2 sts, k2.
Row 3: K2, m1, k to last 4 sts, k2tog, k2.
Row 4: K2, p to last 2 sts, k2.
Rep rows 2–3 twice more.
Row 9: Knit to last 4 sts, ssk, k2. *(13 sts)*
Row 10: K2, p to last 2 sts, k2.
Rep rows 9–10 once more. *(12 sts)*
Rep from * to end to complete second fin.

To make up

Using black yarn, work two coils of chain stitch (see page 124) for the eyes and a rounded triangular shape for the nose. Using a separated strand of black yarn, work a few straight stitches (see page 124) for the whiskers around the nose and on the eyebrows.
Weave in all loose ends.

CHAPTER 4
wild animals

Sassy racoons, impertinent monkeys, slinky snakes, trunk-swinging elephants, and even an elegant flamingo. Whatever your taste in creatures, there are scarves and cowls in this collection that will have you head-over-heels in love. So why sit around twiddling your fingers when you can use them to get creative?

flamingo scarf

The pink flamingo is a pop culture icon. Normally made from pink plastic and adorning gardens or the walls of a retro cocktail bar, now is your chance to create a wool version. This scarf is knitted in two yarns held together, a standard wool and a beautifully fluffy mohair yarn that will give your scarf a lovely feather-soft feel. Wrap it around your neck instead of a feather boa and set a new trend.

Yarn and materials

Patons Merino Extrafine Aran (100% wool) worsted (Aran) yarn

1 x 1¾oz (50g) ball (93yd/85m) in shade 00299 Black (A)

1 x 1¾oz (50g) ball (93yd/85m) in shade 00202 Cream (B)

Patons Merino Extrafine DK (100% wool) light worsted (DK) yarn

2 x 1¾oz (50g) balls (131yd/120m) in shade 00134 Coral (C)

Wendy Air (70% kid mohair, 30% nylon) lace weight yarn

1 x ¾oz (25g) ball (219yd/200m) in shade 2621 Mia (D)

Needles and equipment

US 9 (5.5mm) knitting needles

Yarn sewing needle

Large-eyed embroidery needle

Gauge (tension)

17 sts and 20 rows in stockinette (stocking) stitch to a 4-in (10-cm) square on US 9 (5.5mm) needles using C and D held together.

Measurements

The finished scarf is 63in (160cm) long.

Abbreviations

See page 126.

To make scarf

Cast on 2 sts in A.

Row 1: [Inc] twice. *(4 sts)*

Row 2: Purl.

Row 3: [Inc, k1] twice. *(6 sts)*

Row 4: Purl.

Row 5: Inc, k to last 2 sts, inc, k1. *(8 sts)*

Row 6: Purl.

Rep rows 5–6, 6 times more. *(20 sts)*

Row 19: Knit.

Row 20: Purl.

Break A and join in B.

Knit 6 rows.

Break B and join in C and D, using both yarns held together. The rest of the scarf is knitted in these yarns only.

Row 27: Knit.

Row 28: K2, p to last 2 sts, k2.

Rep last 2 rows, 126 times more.

Shape tail

Row 281: K7, turn. Work on 7 sts just knitted only, leaving rem sts on needle.

***Next row:** K2, p to last 2 sts, k2.

Next row: K3, [k1, p1, k1 all into next st], k3. *(9 sts)*

Next row: K2, p to last 2 sts, k2.

Next row: Ssk, k2, [k1, p1, k1 all into next st], k2, k2tog.

Next row: K2, p to last 2 sts, k2.

Rep last 2 rows, 10 times more.**

Next row: Ssk, k to last 2 sts, k2tog. *(7 sts)*

Next row: P2tog, p3, p2tog. *(5 sts)*

Next row: Ssk, k1, k2tog. *(3 sts)*

Next row: P3tog.

Break yarn and fasten off.***

Rejoin yarn to rem sts on RS of work.

Next row: K3, m1, k3, turn. Work on 7 sts just knitted only, leaving rem sts on needle.

Rep from * to ** once.

Next row: Ssk, k2, [k1, p1, k1 all into next st], k2, k2tog.

Next row: K2, p to last 2 sts, k2.

Rep last 2 rows, 3 times more.

Next row: Ssk, k to last 2 sts, k2tog. *(7 sts)*
Next row: P2tog, p3, p2tog. *(5 sts)*
Next row: Ssk, k1, k2tog. *(3 sts)*
Next row: P3tog. *(1 st)*
Break yarn and fasten off.
Rejoin yarn to rem sts on RS of work.
Next row: Knit.
Rep from * to *** once.

To make up
Using A, embroider two semicircles for
the eyes in chain stitch (see page 124).
Weave in all loose ends.

monkey scarf

This scarf is the perfect knit for the little monkey in your life. It is made in a soft chunky yarn that's quick to knit up and comes in a range of lovely colors. I chose a delightful mauve for this one—for no good reason other than I liked the shade. But you can choose any color you like of course—a fantasy shade or something neutral and more monkey-like.

Yarn and materials

Sirdar Click Chunky with wool (70% acrylic, 30% wool) bulky (chunky) yarn

3 x 1¾oz (50g) balls (81yd/75m) in shade 0131 Heather (A)

Wendy Merino Chunky (100% wool) bulky (chunky) yarn

1 x 1¾oz (50g) ball (71yd/65m) in shade 2471 Latte (B)

Small amounts of black, off-white, and red light worsted (DK) yarn

Needles and equipment

US 10½ (6.5mm) knitting needles

Yarn sewing needle

Large-eyed embroidery needle

Gauge (tension)

14 sts and 19 rows in stockinette (stocking) stitch to a 4-in (10-cm) square on US 10½ (6.5mm) needles.

Measurements

The finished scarf is 39½in (100cm) long, including back legs.

Abbreviations

See page 126.

To make scarf

Cast on 14 sts in A.

Row 1: Inc, k to last 2 sts, inc, k1. *(16 sts)*

Row 2: Purl.

Row 3: K1, m1, k to last st, m1, k1. *(18 sts)*

Row 4: Purl.

Rep rows 3–4 once more. *(20 sts)*

Beg with a k row, work 15 rows in st st.

Row 22: Knit.

Row 23: K2, p to last 2 sts, k2.

Rep rows 22–23, 67 times more.

Knit 6 rows.

Shape back legs

Row 164: K6, bind (cast) off 8 sts, k to end.

Work on 6 sts just knitted only, leaving rem sts on needle.

Knit 9 rows.

Beg with a k row, work 14 rows in st st.

Shape paw

Next row: K2, turn and work on these 2 sts only, leaving rem sts on needle.

*Beg with a p row, work 5 rows in st st.

Next row: K2tog, break yarn and fasten off.**

[Rejoin yarn, knit next 2 sts and rep from * to **] twice more.

Rejoin yarn to 6 rem sts on WS of work and work second leg as for first leg.

Face

Before you start, cut a 12-in (30-cm) length of A.

Cast on 14 sts in A.

Row 1: Inc, k to last 2 sts, inc, k1. *(16 sts)*

Row 2: Purl.

Row 3: K1, m1, k3 in A; join B and k8; k3, m1, k1 in A using yarn from center of ball. *(18 sts)*

Row 4: P4 in A; p10 in B; p4 in A.

Row 5: K1, m1, k2 in A; k12 in B; k2, m1, k1 in A. *(20 sts)*

Row 6: P3 in A; p14 in B; p3 in A.

Row 7: K3 in A; k14 in B; k3 in A.

Rep rows 6–7, 3 times more.

Row 14: P4 in A; p12 in B; p4 in A.

Row 15: K4 in A; k5 in B; using separate 12-in (30-cm) length of A, k2; k5 in B; k4 in A.

Row 16: P5 in A; p3 in B; p4 in A; p3 in B; p5 in A.

Break all yarns except the A you will use to begin next row.

Beg with a k row, work 4 rows in st st.

Bind (cast) off.

Front limbs

Make 2

Cast on 6 sts in A.

Knit 12 rows.

Beg with a k row, work 24 rows in st st.

Shape paw

Row 37: K2, turn and work on these 2 sts only, leaving rem sts on needle.

*Beg with a p row, work 5 rows in st st.

Next row: K2tog, break yarn and fasten off.**

[Rejoin yarn, knit next 2 sts and rep from * to **] twice more.

Ear

Make 2

Cast on 6 sts in A.

Row 1: Inc, k to last 2 sts, inc, k1. *(8 sts)*

Row 2: Purl.

Row 3: K1, m1, k to last st, m1, k1. *(10 sts)*

Row 4: Purl.

Rep last 2 rows once more.

Bind (cast) off quite tightly.

Tail

Cast on 8 sts in A.

Beg with a k row, work 64 rows in st st.

Row 65: Ssk, k4, k2tog. *(6 sts)*

Row 66: P2tog, p2, p2tog. *(4 sts)*

Break yarn, thread it through rem sts, and pull up securely.

To make up

On the face, using black yarn, embroider two small circles using chain stitch (see page 124) for the center of the eyes. Work a circle of chain stitch around the eye centers using off-white yarn. Using black yarn, work two straight stitches (see page 124) for the nose. Using red yarn, work the mouth in chain stitch. Weave in ends of yarns on back of face.

Place the face on the head part of the main scarf so that the right sides are together. Oversew (see page 125) the side and chin seams. Turn the head the right way out and sew the top edge in place using mattress stitch (see page 125).

Oversew the front legs in place underneath the head, where the head meets the main part of the scarf.

Oversew the ears in place on the side of the head using the photograph as a guide.

Join the long seam of the tail using flat stitch (see page 125). Sew the tail in place on the monkey's lower end, just where the garter stitch border meets the main part of the scarf. Weave in all loose ends.

snake socks

Soft and snuggly… not the first words you think about when you say "snake," except when you're talking about these lovely socks. They're knitted in a 100% wool yarn, to make sure they're really cozy. For a change—and for knitters who don't like working on double-pointed or circular needles—these socks are knitted on straight needles. (You have to sew a seam at the back when you've finished, but with the flat seam technique this is barely visible.) I fancied knitting these stripy snakes in pale blue with a contrasting raspberry-pink stripe, but you can knit them in whatever color takes your fancy.

skill level

Yarn and materials

Rowan Pure Wool DK (100% wool) light worsted (DK) yarn
1 x 1¾oz (50g) ball (142yd/130m) in shade 028
Raspberry (A)
2 x 1¾oz (50g) balls (142yd/130m) in shade 00058
Cloud (B)
Small amount of light worsted (DK) yarn in off-white (C)
Small amount of light worsted (DK) yarn in mid-green (D)
Small amount of light worsted (DK) yarn in black
A handful of 100% polyester toy filling

Needles and equipment

US 8 (5mm) knitting needles
US 6 (4mm) knitting needles
US 5 (3.75mm) knitting needles
A G/6 (4mm) or similar size crochet hook
Yarn sewing needle
Large-eyed embroidery needle

Gauge (tension)

22 sts and 30 rows in stockinette (stocking) stich to a 4-in (10-cm) square on US 6 (4mm) needles.

Measurements

The finished socks measure 6¾in (17cm) from the heel to the tip of the toe. They should fit a child's shoe size US 11½–12½ (UK 10½–11½/EU 29–30)

Abbreviations

See page 126.

To make socks

Make 2

Using US 8 (5mm) needles, cast on 44 sts in A.
Change to US 6 (4 mm) needles.
Row 1: [K2, p2] to end.
Rep row 1, 9 times more.
Leave A at side of work and join in B.
Beg with a k row, work 4 rows in st st.
Leave B at side of work and use A.
Beg with a k row, work 2 rows in st st.
Rep last 6 rows, 7 times more.
Break A and work remainder of sock in B.
Beg with a k row, work 4 rows in st st.
Shape heel
Row 63: K12, turn and work on these 12 sts only, leaving rem sts on needle.
Beg with a p row, work 13 rows in st st.
Next row: K2, k2tog, k1, turn.
Next row: Sl1, p3.
Next row: K3, k2tog, k1, turn.
Next row: Sl1, p4.
Next row: K4, k2tog, k1, turn.
Next row: Sl1, p5.
Next row: K5, k2tog, k1, turn.
Next row: Sl1, p6.
Next row: K6, k2tog. *(7 sts)*
Using right-hand needle, pick up and knit 10 sts up side of heel part just worked. Knit across rem sts. *(49 sts)*
Next row: P12, turn and work on these 12 sts only.
Beg with a k row, work 11 rows on these 12 sts, beg with a k row.
Next row: P2, p2tog, p1, turn.
Next row: Sl1, k3.
Next row: P3, p2tog, p1, turn.
Next row: Sl1, k4.

Next row: P4, p2tog, p1, turn.
Next row: Sl1, k5.
Next row: P5, p2tog, p1, turn.
Next row: Sl1, k6.
Next row: P6, p2tog. *(7 sts)*
Pick up and purl 10 sts on side of heel part just worked, p rem sts on left-hand needle. *(54 sts)*
Shape foot
Row 1: K15, k2tog, k20, ssk, k15. *(52 sts)*
Row 2 and every WS row: Purl.
Row 3: K14, k2tog, k20, ssk, k14. *(50 sts)*
Row 5: K13, k2tog, k20, ssk, k13. *(48 sts)*
Row 7: K12, k2tog, k20, ssk, k12. *(46 sts)*
Row 9: K11, k2tog, k20, ssk, k11. *(44 sts)*
Row 11: K10, k2tog, k20, ssk, k10. *(42 sts)*
Row 13: K9, k2tog, k20, ssk, k9. *(40 sts)*
Row 15: K8, k2tog, k20, ssk, k8. *(38 sts)*
Row 16: Purl.
Beg with a k row, work 14 rows in st st.
Shape toe
Row 31: K7, k2tog, k1, ssk, k14, k2tog, k1, ssk, k7. *(34 sts)*
Row 32 and every WS row: Purl.
Row 33: K6, k2tog, k1, ssk, k12, k2tog, k1, ssk, k6. *(30 sts)*
Row 35: K5, k2tog, k1, ssk, k10, k2tog, k1, ssk, k5. *(26 sts)*
Row 37: K4, k2tog, k1, ssk, k8, k2tog, k1, ssk, k4. *(22 sts)*
Row 39: K3, k2tog, k1, ssk, k6, k2tog, k1, ssk, k3. *(18 sts)*
(End your work on row 39, without working a purl row.)
Break yarn, thread it through rem sts, and pull up securely.

Eye hoods
Make 4
Using US 5 (3.75mm) needles, cast on 3 sts in B.
Row 1: [Inc] 3 times. *(6 sts)*

Row 2: Knit.
Row 3: K1, [m1, k1] to end. *(11 sts)*
Row 4: Knit.
Bind (cast) off.

Eyeballs
Make 4
Using US 5 (3.75mm) needles, cast on 3 sts in C.
Row 1: [Inc] 3 times. *(6 sts)*
Row 2: Purl.
Row 3: [Inc] 6 times. *(12 sts)*
Row 4: Purl.
Row 5: [K2tog] to end. *(6 sts)*
Row 6: [P2tog] to end. *(3 sts)*
Break yarn, thread it through rem sts, and pull up securely.

Tongue
Make 2
Using the crochet hook and D, work a 3½-in (9-cm) chain, leaving long yarn tails.

To make up
Join the back seam of sock using flat stitch (see page 125). Sew the eye hoods in place so that the bound- (cast-) off edges form the outer rim of the eye hood. Join the side seam of the eyeballs using flat stitch, stuffing lightly as you go. Place the eyeballs in the eye hoods. Stitch in place along the part of the eyeball that meets the top of the foot and along the outer rim of the eye hood.
Using black yarn, work a small circle of chain stitch (see page 124) for the eye centers.
Run one of the yarn tails on the crochet chain to the center. Do the same with the second yarn tail, stopping about ½in (1cm) before the center and using the yarn tail to join the two parts of the chain together to form the forked shape.
Join the tongue to the end of the sock.
Weave in all loose ends.

> **here's a tip** *When sewing something striped, remember to make sure the stripes line up across the seam. This will help you sew the seam evenly, and will give your stripes a very professional finish.*

koala scarf

Who can resist this big-nosed marsupial from Australia? Well now you can create your own wooly version of this cuddly looking eucalyptus muncher in the shape of a scarf. I've knitted this one in a beautifully soft alpaca-rich yarn, but it would work well in almost any good quality yarn. The yarn is chunky in weight, there aren't too many stitches, and the pattern is simple, so you'll find your project will grow pretty quickly. What are you waiting for? Get your needles out now and start knitting.

Yarn and materials

Bergere de France Alpaga (60% merino, 40% alpaca) bulky (chunky) yarn

2 x 1¾oz (50g) balls (71yd/65m) in shade 29908 Grey (A)

1 x 1¾oz (50g) ball (71yd/65m) in shade 29899 Ecru (B)

Small amount of light worsted (DK) yarn in black (C)

A handful of 100% polyester toy filling

Needles and equipment

US 10½ (6.5mm) knitting needles

Yarn sewing needle

Large-eyed embroidery needle

A pompom maker to make 3½in (9cm) pompoms, or two cardboard circles each measuring 3½in (9cm) in diameter with a 1½in (4cm) diameter hole in the center

Gauge (tension)

14 sts and 18 rows in stockinette (stocking) stitch to a 4-in (10-cm) square on US 10½ (6.5mm) needles.

Measurements

The finished scarf is 46½in (118cm) long.

Abbreviations

See page 126.

To make scarf

Cast on 14 sts in A.

Row 1: Inc, k to last st, inc, k1. *(16 sts)*

Row 2: Purl.

Row 3: K1, m1, k to last st, m1, k1. *(18 sts)*

Row 4: Purl.

Rep rows 3–4 once more. *(20 sts)*

Beg with a k row, work 15 rows in st st.

Row 22: Knit.

Row 23: K3, p to last 3 sts, k3.

Rep rows 22–23, 84 times more.

Knit 6 rows.

Shape back legs

Row 198: K6, bind (cast) off 8 sts, k to end.

Cont on 6 sts just knitted only, leaving rem sts on needle.

Knit 13 rows.

Shape paw

Break A and join in C, using yarn double.

Knit 4 rows.

Next row: K2, turn and work on these 2 sts just knitted only, leaving rem sts on needle.

*Knit 3 rows.

Next row: Skpo, [pick up and knit 1 st from row ends, bind (cast) off 1 st] 3 times, k1 from left-hand needle, bind (cast) off 1 st, k1. *(2 sts)*

Rep from * once more.

Knit 3 rows.

Next row: Skpo. *(1 st)*

Break yarn and fasten off.

Rejoin A to rem 6 sts on needle on WS of work.

Knit 13 rows.

Break A and join in C, using yarn double.

Shape paw as for first back leg.

Front leg

Make 2

Cast on 6 sts in A.

Knit 36 rows.

Break A and join in C, using yarn double.

Shape paw as for back legs.

Face

Cast on 14 sts in A.

Row 1: Inc, k to last st, inc, k1. *(16 sts)*

Row 2: Purl.

Row 3: K1, m1, k to last st, m1, k1. *(18 sts)*

Row 4: Purl.

Rep rows 3–4 once more. *(20 sts)*

Beg with a k row, work 14 rows in st st.

Bind (cast) off.

Ear

Make 4; 2 in A and 2 in B

Cast on 8 sts.

Beg with a k row, work 4 rows in st st.

Row 5: Ssk, k4, k2tog. *(6 sts)*

Row 6: P2tog, p2, p2tog. *(4 sts)*

Bind (cast) off.

To make up

On the face, using C, embroider two small circles using chain stitch (see page 124) for the centers of the eyes. Using B, work a circle of chain stitch around the eye centers. Using C and chain stitch, work large oval shape for the nose. The oval should be approximately 1¼in (3cm) wide and 1¾in (4cm) long.

Place the face on the head part of the main scarf so that the right sides are together. Oversew (see page 125) the side seams. Turn the head the right way out and sew the top edge in place using mattress stitch (see page 125).

Oversew the front legs in place underneath the head, where the head meets the main part of the scarf.

Place two ear pieces together, one in A and one in B, so that the right sides are on the inside. Oversew around the curved edge leaving the flat edges open for turning. Turn the piece the right way out. Make the second ear in the same way. Stuff the ears very lightly and sew them in place on the side of the head using the photograph as a guide.

For the tail, make a pompom using B and the pompom maker or cardboard circles. Sew the pompom in place just above the garter stitch border at the lower end of the scarf. Weave in all loose ends.

here's a tip *You can buy plastic pompom makers at quite reasonable prices. They are simple to use and make creating pompoms really easy. For the best value, look out for sets with makers in a range of sizes.*

tiger cowl

For those days when you want something simple, a wooly cowl is the perfect solution. But why have something plain when with just a miniscule amount of effort you could join the animal print revolution and whip up a tiger print version? I've knitted this cowl in really tigery shades. And as if that wasn't enough, I've brushed up the yarn to give it a really furry feel.

Yarn

Sirdar Click DK (70% acrylic, 30% wool) light worsted (DK) yarn

1 x 1¾oz (50g) ball (164yd/150m) in shade 188 Rustica (A)

Sirdar Country Style DK (40% nylon, 30% wool, 30% acrylic) light worsted (DK) yarn

1 x 1¾oz (50g) ball (170yd/155m) in shade 417 Black (B)

Needles and equipment

US 10½ (6.5mm) knitting needles

Yarn sewing needle

Gauge (tension)

13 sts and 17 rows in stockinette (stocking) stitch to a 4-in (10-cm) square on US 10½ (6.5mm) needles for both yarns, using yarn double.

Measurements

The finished cowl measures 21½in (55cm) circumference and is 9½in (24cm) deep.

Abbreviations

See page 126.

To make scarf

First, wind off 12 x 11-yd (10-m) lengths of B.

Use all yarns double throughout.

Cast on 72 sts in A.

Row 1: Knit.

Beg with a k row, work 4 rows in st st.

Break A and join in a length of B.

Row 6: K42 in B; rejoin A and k to end.

Row 7: P28 in A; p in B to end.

Row 8: K42 in B; k in A to end.

Row 9: Purl in A.

Row 10: Knit in A.

Break A and join in a length of B.

Row 11: P42 in B; rejoin A and p to end.

Row 12: K28 in A; k in B to end.

Row 13: P42 in B; p in A to end.

Row 14: Knit in A.

Row 15: Purl in A.

Break A and join in a length of B.

Row 16: K38 in B; rejoin A and k to end.

Row 17: P31 in A; p in B to end.

Row 18: K38 in B; k in A to end.

Row 19: Purl in A.

Row 20: Knit in A.

Break A and join in a length of B.

Row 21: P38 in B; rejoin A and p to end.

Row 22: K32 in A; k in B to end.

Row 23: P38 in B; p in A to end.

Row 24: Knit in A.

Row 25: Purl in A.

Break A and join in a length of B.

Rep rows 6–15 once more but do not break A after row 15.

Work remainder of cowl in A.

Beg with a k row, work 6 rows in st st.

Bind (cast) off.

To make up

Sew back seam of cowl using flat stitch (see page 125).

Weave in all loose ends.

To make your cowl look furry, dampen thoroughly, brush carefully using a nylon nail brush, or similar, and let dry.

racoon scarf

Classically dressed in his coat of black, gray, and white—and with a reputation for making mischief—it's no wonder racoons are so appealing. But with this racoon, you won't have to worry about your food being raided, or about any sharp claws. The classic colors will complement almost any outfit—so what are you waiting for? It's time to hunt down those needles and hit the yarn store.

Yarn

King Cole Magnum Lightweight Chunky
(75% acrylic, 25% wool) bulky (chunky) yarn
1 x 3½oz (100g) ball (120yd/110m) in shade 010
Champagne (A)
2 x 3½oz (100g) balls (120yd/110m) in shade 349
Graphite (B)
1 x 3½oz (100g) ball (120yd/110m) in shade 187
Charcoal (C)

Needles and equipment

US 10 (6mm) knitting needles
Yarn sewing needle
Large-eyed embroidery needle

Gauge (tension)

14 sts and 20 rows in stockinette (stocking) stitch
to a 4-in (10-cm) square on US 10 (6mm) needles.

Measurements

The finished scarf is 55in (140cm) long, including back legs.

Abbreviations

See page 126.

To make scarf

Cast on 2 sts in A.
Row 1: [Inc] twice. *(4 sts)*
Row 2: Purl.
Row 3: K1, m1, k2, m1, k1. *(6 sts)*
Row 4: Purl.
Row 5: K1, m1, k to last st, m1, k1. *(8 sts)*
Row 6: Purl.
Rep rows 5–6 twice more. *(12 sts)*
Break A and join in B.
Rep rows 5–6, 5 times more. *(22 sts)*
Beg with a k row, work 5 rows in st st.
Row 26: Knit.
Row 27: K3, p to last 3 sts, k3.
Rep rows 26–27, 107 times.
Knit 6 rows.
Shape back legs
Row 248: K6, bind (cast) off 10 sts, k to end.
Work on 6 sts just knitted, leaving rem sts on needle.
*Knit 11 rows.
Break B and join in C.
Beg with a k row, work 16 rows in st st.
Shape paw
Next row: Ssk, k2, k2tog. *(4 sts)*
Next row: [P2tog] twice. *(2 sts)*
Next row: K2tog. *(1 st)*
Break yarn and fasten off. **
Rejoin B to rem 6 sts on WS of work.
Rep from * to ** once more.

Face

Cast on 2 sts in A.
Row 1: [Inc] twice. *(4 sts)*
Row 2: Purl.
Row 3: K1, m1, k2, m1, k1. *(6 sts)*
Row 4: Purl.
Row 5: K1, m1, k to last st, m1, k1. *(8 sts)*
Row 6: Purl.

Shape paw

Row 33: Ssk, k2, k2tog. *(4 sts)*

Row 34: [P2tog] twice. *(2 sts)*

Row 35: K2tog. *(1 st)*

Break yarn and fasten off.

Tail

Cast on 6 sts in B.

Row 1: Inc, k to last 2 sts, inc, k1. *(8 sts)*

Beg with a p row, work 3 rows in st st.

Leave B at side of work and join in C.

Row 5: K2, m1, k to last 2 sts, m1, k2. *(10 sts)*

Beg with a p row, work 3 rows in st st.

Leave C at side of work and use B.

Row 9: K3, m1, k to last 3 sts, m1, k3. *(12 sts)*

Beg with a p row, work 3 rows in st st.

Leave B at side of work and use C.

Row 13: K3, m1, k to last 3 sts, m1, k3. *(14 sts)*

Beg with a p row, work 3 rows in st st.

Leave C at side of work and use B.

Row 17: K4, m1, k to last 4 sts, m1, k4. *(16 sts)*

Beg with a p row, work 3 rows in st st.

Leave B at side of work and use C.

Row 21: K4, m1, k to last 4 sts, m1, k4. *(18 sts)*

Beg with a p row, work 3 rows in st st.

Leave C at side of work and use B.

Row 25: K5, m1, k to last 5 sts, m1, k5. *(20 sts)*

Beg with a p row, work 3 rows in st st.

Leave B at side of work and use C.

Row 29: K5, m1, k to last 5 sts, m1, k5. *(22 sts)*

Beg with a p row, work 3 rows in st st.

Leave C at side of work and use B.

Beg with a k row, work 4 rows in st st.

Leave B at side of work and use C.

Beg with a k row, work 4 rows in st st.

Leave C at side of work and use B.

Row 41: K5, ssk, k8, k2tog, k to end. *(20 sts)*

Row 42: Purl.

Row 43: K4, ssk, k8, k2tog, k to end. *(18 sts)*

Row 44: Purl.

Rep rows 5–6 twice more. *(12 sts)*

Break A and join in C.

Rep rows 5–6, 3 times more. *(18 sts)*

Break C and join in A.

Rep rows 5–6 twice more. *(22 sts)*

Break A and join in B.

Beg with a k row, work 4 rows in st st.

Bind (cast) off.

Ear

Make 2

Cast on 6 sts in B.

Beg with a k row, work 4 rows in st st.

Row 5: Ssk, k2, k2tog. *(4 sts)*

Row 6: [P2tog] twice. *(2 sts)*

Row 7: K2tog. *(1 st)*

Row 8: Inc pwise. *(2 sts)*

Row 9: [Inc] twice. *(4 sts)*

Row 10: Purl.

Row 11: K1, m1, k2, m1, k1. *(6 sts)*

Beg with a p row, work 4 rows in st st.

Bind (cast) off.

Front leg

Make 2

Cast on 6 sts in B.

Knit 14 rows.

Break B and join in C.

Beg with a k row, work 18 rows in st st beg with a k row.

> **here's a tip** *Some knitters find that they bind (cast) off too tightly and their work looks pulled. If this sounds like you, try using a needle a couple of sizes larger when binding off, and check the edge as you go.*

Leave B at side of work and use C.
Row 45: K4, ssk, k6, k2tog, k to end. *(16 sts)*
Row 46: Purl.
Row 47: K3, ssk, k6, k2tog, k to end. *(14 sts)*
Row 48: Purl.
Leave C at side of work and use B.
Row 49: K3, ssk, k4, k2tog, k to end. *(12 sts)*
Row 50: Purl.
Row 51: K2, ssk, k4, k2tog, k to end. *(10 sts)*
Row 52: Purl.
Break B and work remainder of tail in C.
Row 53: K2, ssk, k2, k2tog, k2. *(8 sts)*
Row 54: Purl.
Row 55: K1, ssk, k2, k2tog, k1. *(6 sts)*
Row 56: P2tog, p2, p2tog. *(4 sts)*
Row 57: Ssk, k2tog. *(2 sts)*
Row 58: P2tog. *(1 st)*
Break yarn and fasten off.

To make up

On the face, using a separated strand of A, embroider two circles in chain stitch (see page 124) for the eyes.
Place the face on the head part of the main scarf so that the right sides are together. Oversew (see page 125) the side seams. Turn the head the right way out and sew the top edge in place using mattress stitch (see page 125). Using a separated strand of C, embroider a coil of chain stitch around the lower pointed end of the face for the nose.
Oversew the front legs in place underneath the head, where the head meets the main part of the scarf.
Fold the ears in half so that the right sides are on the inside and oversew around the sides, leaving the lower (cast-on and bound-/cast- off edges) open for turning. Turn the ears and oversew the lower edges. Oversew the ears in place at the top of the head using the photograph as a guide.
Sew the back seam of the tail using flat stitch (see page 125). Oversew the tail in place in the center of the racoon's lower end, making sure the seam is in the center, just where the garter stitch border meets the main part of the scarf.
Weave in all loose ends.

rattlesnake scarf

Not everyone would welcome the opportunity of draping a snake around their neck, unless, of course, it's this super-soft and wooly rattlesnake scarf. The pattern is very easy to do, so forget all those worries about two-color knitting; I guarantee you'll find this two-color knitting easy enough not to cause a worry—and just challenging enough to keep you interested. I love the colors we've chosen here, but the scarf will work brilliantly in any number of color combinations. So have a look around at what's available and choose a duo you adore.

Yarn
Katia Peru (40% wool, 40% acrylic, 20% alpaca) bulky (chunky) yarn
1 x 3½oz (100g) ball (116yd/106m) in shade 028 (A)
King Cole Magnum Lightweight Chunky (25% wool, 75% acrylic) bulky (chunky) yarn
1 x 3½oz (100g) ball (120yd/110m) in shade 316 Pebble (B)
Small amount of bulky (chunky) yarn in cream (C)
Small amounts of black and coral light worsted (DK) yarn
Small handful of 100% polyester toy filling

Needles and equipment
US 10½ (6.5mm) needles
A J/10 (6mm) or similar size crochet hook
Yarn sewing needle
Large-eyed embroidery needle

Gauge (tension)
12 sts and 16 rows in stockinette (stocking) stitch to a 4-in (10-cm) square on US 10½ (6.5mm) needles for both yarns.

Measurements
The finished scarf is 70½in (179cm) long, including the knotted tail.

Abbreviations
See page 126(.

To make scarf
Cast on 7 sts in A.
Row 1: Inc, k to last 2 sts, inc, k1. *(9 sts)*
Row 2: Knit.
Row 3: Inc, k to last 2 sts, inc, k1. *(11 sts)*
Row 4: K2, p to last 2 sts, k2.
Row 5: K1, m1, k to last st, m1, k1. *(13 sts)*
Row 6: K2, p to last 2 sts, k2.
Rep last 2 rows, 4 times more. *(21 sts)*
Row 15: Knit.
Row 16: K2, p to last 2 sts, k2.
Rep rows 15–16, 3 times more.
Leave A at side of work and join in B.
Row 23: K2 in B, [k1 in A, k1 in B] to last 3 sts, k1 in A, k2 in B.

Row 1: [Inc] twice, k1. *(5 sts)*
Row 2: Knit.
Row 3: K1, [m1, k1] to end. *(9 sts)*
Row 4: Knit.
Bind (cast) off.

Eyeballs
Make 2
Cast on 3 sts in C.
Row 1: [Inc] 3 times. *(6 sts)*
Row 2: Purl.
Row 3: K1, [m1, k1] to end. *(11 sts)*
Row 4: Purl.
Row 5: [K2tog] twice, sl1, k2tog, psso, [ssk] twice. *(5 sts)*
Break yarn, thread it through rem sts, and pull up securely.

Tongue
Using the crochet hook and the coral light worsted (DK) yarn double, work a 5-in (13-cm) crochet chain.

To make up
Sew the eye hoods in place so that the bound- (cast-) off edges form the outer rim of the eye hood. Join the side seam of the eyeballs using flat stitch (see page 125), stuffing lightly as you go. Place the eyeballs in the eye hoods. Stitch in place along the part of the eyeball that meets the main scarf and along the outer rim of the eye hood. Using three strands of black DK yarn, work three long straight stitches (see page 124) for the eye centers. Thread the crochet chain for the tongue through the tip of the head and match the two ends. Sew the first ¾in (2cm) of the strands, nearest to the head, together to form the forked end.
Make a knot in the end of the tail.
Weave in all loose ends.

Row 24: In B, k2, p to last 2 sts, k2.
Row 25: In B, knit.
Row 26: K2 in B, [p1 in A, p1 in B] to last 3 sts, p1 in A, k2 in B.
Row 27: In A, knit.
Row 28: In A, k2, p to last 2 sts, k2.
Rep rows 23–28, 36 times more.
Rep rows 23–24 once more.
Break A and work remainder of scarf in B.
Row 247: K2, ssk, k to last 4 sts, k2tog, k2. *(19 sts)*
Row 248: K2, p to last 2 sts, k2.
Row 249: Knit.
Row 250: Purl.
Rep rows 247–250, 5 times more. *(9 sts)*
Row 271: K2, ssk, k1, k2tog, k2. *(7 sts)*
Row 272: K2, p to last 2 sts, k2.
Row 273: Knit.
Row 274: K2, p to last 2 sts, k2.
Row 275: K1, ssk, k1, k2tog, k1. *(5 sts)*
Knit 25 rows.
Row 301: Ssk, k1, k2tog. *(3 sts)*
Row 302: Sl1, k2tog, psso. *(1 st)*
Break yarn and fasten off.

Eye hoods
Make 2
Cast on 3 sts in A.

here's a tip
If you find the edges of your scarf tend to curl in, don't panic. All you need to do is soak the completed project in lukewarm water, stretch the sides gently, and dry the scarf flat.

elephant scarf

Elephants are my favorite animal—and baby elephants are simply gorgeous. If you feel like I do, you can now knit your very own baby elephant scarf. I've chosen a beautiful 100% wool yarn in a lovely blueish gray for this version. But I also think he would look just as lovely in pale gray, or even pink. An elephant scarf to match every outfit perhaps?

Yarn
Wendy Merino Chunky (100% wool) bulky (chunky) yarn
3 x 1¾oz (50g) ball (71yd/65m) in shade 2483
Periwinkle (A)
Patons Merino Extrafine DK (100% wool) light worsted (DK) yarn
1 x 1¾oz (50g) ball (131yd/120m) in shade 00101 White (B)
Small amount of black light worsted (DK) yarn

Needles and equipment
US 10½ (6.5mm) knitting needles
US 9 (5.5mm) knitting needles
Yarn sewing needle
Large-eyed embroidery needle

Gauge (tension)
14 sts and 19 rows in stockinette (stocking) stitch to a 4-in (10-cm) square on US 10½ (6.5mm) needles using A.

Measurements
The finished scarf is 41½in (105cm) long, including trunk and back legs.

Abbreviations
See page 126.

To make scarf
Using US 10½ (6.5mm) needles, cast on 7 sts in A.
Row 1: Knit.
Row 2: Purl.
Rep rows 1–2, 10 times more.
Row 23: Cast on 4 sts, k to end. *(11 sts)*
Row 24: Cast on 4 sts, p to end. *(15 sts)*
Rep rows 23–24 once more. *(23 sts)*
Row 27: Knit.
Row 28: Purl.
Rep rows 27–28, 8 times more.
Row 45: Knit.
Row 46: Knit.
Row 47: K2, p to last 2 sts, k2.
Rep rows 46–47, 68 times more.
Knit 6 rows.
Shape back legs
Row 190: K7, bind (cast) off 9 sts, k to end.

Rep rows 27–28, 8 times more.
Bind (cast) off.

Ears

First ear
Using US 10½ (6.5mm) needles, cast on 15 sts in A.
Knit 6 rows.*
Row 7: K1, k2tog, k to end. *(14 sts)*
Row 8: Knit.
Rep rows 7–8, 3 times more. *(11 sts)*
Row 15: K1, k2tog, k5, ssk, k1. *(9 sts)*
Bind (cast) off.
Second ear
Work as for first ear to *.
Row 7: Knit to last 3 sts, ssk, k1.
Row 8: Knit.
Rep rows 7–8, 3 times more. *(11 sts)*
Row 15: K1, k2tog, k5, ssk, k1. *(9 sts)*
Bind (cast) off.

Tusks

Make 2
Using US 9 (5.5mm) needles, cast on 5 sts using B double.
Knit 10 rows.
Row 11: Ssk, k1, k2tog. *(3 sts)*
Break yarn, thread it through rem sts, and pull securely.

Tail

Using US 10½ (6.5mm) needles, cast on 12 sts in A.
Bind (cast) off.

To make up

For the eyes, work a curved line of chain stitch (see page 124) in black yarn. For the eyelashes, separate a length of the black yarn and work 5 straight stitches (see page 124) along each eye curve. Join seam of tusk and sew in place.
Place the face on the head part of the main scarf so that the right sides are together. Oversew (see page 125) the side seams and around the trunk. Turn the head the right way out and sew the top edge in place using mattress stitch (see page 125).
On the ears, thread the tail of cast-on edge around the outer edge of the ears to the bound- (cast-) off edge. Pull gently to curve the edge slightly and secure. Stitch the ears in place using the photograph as a guide.
Sew the tail in place using yarn tails just at the beginning of the garter stitch border. For the tassel on the end of the tail, thread three 4-in (10-cm) lengths of yarn through and tie securely. Separate yarn threads and trim.
Weave in all loose ends.

Work on group of 7 sts just worked only, leaving rem sts on needle.
Knit 15 rows.
Next row: Ssk, k3, k2tog. *(5 sts)*
Bind (cast) off.
With WS facing, rejoin yarn to second group of 7 sts.
Knit 15 rows.
Next row: Ssk, k3, k2tog. *(5 sts)*
Bind (cast) off.

Face

Using US 10½ (6.5mm) needles, cast on 7 sts in A.
Row 1: Knit.
Row 2: Purl
Rep rows 1–2, 10 times more.
Row 23: Cast on 4 sts, k to end. *(11 sts)*
Row 24: Cast on 4 sts, p to end. *(15 sts)*
Rep rows 23–24 once more. *(23 sts)*
Row 27: Knit.
Row 28: Purl.

bear scoodie

Is it a scarf? Is it a hat? It's a "scoodie" of course. That's half hood and half scarf to you and me. In fact, this cute bear scoodie is a pair of mitts as well—because when the temperature really plummets, you can keep your hands cozy in the paw-like mitts at the scoodie's two ends. What's not to like? It's worked in a double seed (moss) stitch, so although the texture looks complicated, it's really easy to do. And the super-chunky yarn means that your work grows super-quickly.

Yarn
Lion Brand Wool-Ease Thick & Quick (80% acrylic, 20% wool) super-bulky (super-chunky) yarn
2 x 6oz (170g) balls (106yd/97m) in shade 189 Butterscotch (A)
1 x 6oz (170g) ball (106yd/97m) in shade 135 Spice (B)

Needles and equipment
US 13 (9mm) knitting needles
Yarn sewing needle
4 stitch markers or small safety pins

Gauge (tension)
9 sts and 12 rows in stockinette (stocking) stich to a 4-in (10-cm) square on US 13 (9mm) needles.

Measurements
The finished scoodie is 36in (91cm) from the top center of the head to the bottom of each pocket. The hat part is 18in (46cm) in circumference.

Abbreviations
See page 126.

To make scoodie
Cast on 42 sts in A.
Mark the 5th, 14th, 29th, and 38th cast-on st with a stitch marker or small safety pin.
Row 1: [K1, p1] to end.
Rep row 1 once more.
Row 3: [P1, k1] to end.
Rep row 3 once more.
Rep rows 1–4, 3 times more.
Row 17: [K1, p1] to end.
Row 18: K1, [p2tog, k2tog, p1, k1] 6 times, p2tog, k2tog, p1. *(28 sts)*
Row 19: [P1, k1] to end.
Row 20: [P2tog, k2tog] to end. *(14 sts)*
Row 21: [K2tog, p2tog] to last 2 sts, k2tog. *(7 sts)*
Break yarn, thread it through rem sts, and pull up securely.
With RS facing and using A, pick up and k 10 sts from the first to the second marker on cast-on edge.

Row 1: [K1, p1] to end.
Rep row 1 once more.
Row 3: [P1, k1] to end.
Rep row 3 once more.
Rep rows 1–4, 14 times more
Break A, join in B and work remainder of this part of the scoodie in B.
Rep rows 1–4, 8 times more.
Rep rows 1–2 once more.
Bind (cast) off.
With right side facing and using A, pick up and k 10 sts from the third to the fourth marker.
Rep from * to end.

Ear

Make 4; 2 in A and 2 in B
Cast on 9 sts.
Row 1: [K1, p1] to last st, k1.
Row 2: [P1, k1] to last st, p1.
Row 3: [P1, k1] to last st, p1.
Row 4: [K1, p1] to last st, k1.
Row 5: P2tog, [k1, p1] twice, k1, p2tog. *(7 sts)*
Row 6: P2tog, k1, p1, k1, p2tog. *(5 sts)*
Row 7: K2tog, p1, ssk. *(3 sts)*
Row 8: P3tog. *(1 st)*
Break yarn and fasten off.

To make up

Place two ear pieces together, right sides facing—one in A and one in B. Oversew (see page 125) around curved edge leaving flat edges open for turning. Turn the piece the right way out. Make the second ear in the same way. Sew the ears in place on the hat part of the scoodie using the photograph as a guide.
Fold the pockets upward so that the right sides are on the inside. Oversew the two sides, close to the edge. Turn the pockets the right way out.
Weave in all loose ends.

zebra cowl

Super-simple, super-quick, and super-stylish: what more could you ask for? If you're a newbie knitter, or just fancy working on something quick, this is the perfect project for you. The yarn is super-chunky, so the knitting will grow at a cracking pace. The cowl is generously sized, so it will suit adults as well as older children and teens. And it's soft and cozy, too. I've used classic monochrome zebra stripes, but if you fancy other combinations, who am I to tell you not to?

Yarn
Lion Brand Wool-Ease Thick & Quick (82% acrylic, 10% wool, 8% rayon) super-bulky (super-chunky) yarn
1 x 6oz (170g) ball (108yd/98m) in shade 153 Black (A)
1 x 6oz (170g) ball (108yd/98m) in shade 099 Fisherman (B)

Needles and equipment
US 13 (9mm) knitting needles
Yarn sewing needle

Gauge (tension)
9 sts and 12 rows in stockinette (stocking) stitch in A to a 4-in (10-cm) square on US 13 (9mm) needles.

Measurements
The finished cowl measures 26½in (67cm) in circumference and is 12½in (32cm) deep.

Abbreviations
See page 126.

To make cowl
Cast on 60 sts in A.
Beg with a k row, work 2 rows in st st.
Leave A at side of work and join in B.
Beg with a k row, work 2 rows in st st.
Leave B at side of work and use A.
Beg with a k row, work 2 rows in st st.
Rep rows 2–6 (last 4 rows), 8 times more.
Bind (cast) off.

To make up
Sew back seam of cowl using flat stitch (see page 125).
Weave in all loose ends.

techniques

In this section you'll find the basic knitting techniques that you will need for most of the patterns in this book.

The knitting needles, yarn, and other items that you need are listed at the beginning of each of the pattern instructions. You can substitute the yarn recommended in a pattern with the same weight of yarn in a different brand, but you will need to check the gauge (tension). When calculating the quantity of yarn you require, it is the length of yarn in each ball that you need to check, rather than the weight of the ball; the length of yarn per ball in each recommended project yarn is given in the pattern.

If substituting brands when the amount needed is very small—for example for the embroidery of the nose or the eyes—this will hardly affect the look of your project at all, and it is very sensible to use up the yarns you have in your stash.

Gauge (tension)

A gauge (tension) is given with each pattern to help you make your item the same size as the sample. The gauge is given as the number of stitches and rows you need to work to produce a 4-in (10-cm) square of knitting.

Using the recommended yarn and needles, cast on 8 stitches more than the gauge (tension) instruction asks for—so if you need to have 10 stitches to 4in (10cm), cast on 18 stitches. Working in pattern as instructed, work eight rows more than is needed. Bind (cast) off loosely.

Lay the swatch flat without stretching it. Lay a ruler across the stitches as shown, with the 2in (5cm) mark centered on the knitting, then put a pin in the knitting at the start of the ruler and at the 4in (10cm) mark: the pins should be well away from the edges of the swatch. Count the number of stitches between the pins. Repeat the process across the rows to count the number of rows to 4in (10cm).

If the number of stitches and rows you've counted is the same as the number asked for in the instructions, you have the correct gauge (tension). If you do not have the same number then you will need to change your gauge (tension).

To change gauge (tension) you need to change the size of your knitting needles. A good rule of thumb to follow is that one difference in needle size will create a difference of one stitch in the gauge (tension). You will need to use larger needles to achieve fewer stitches and smaller ones to achieve more stitches.

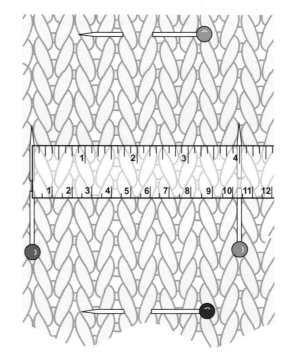

Holding needles

If you are a knitting novice, you will need to discover which is the most comfortable way for you to hold your needles.

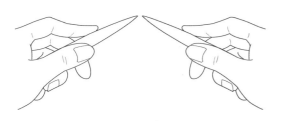

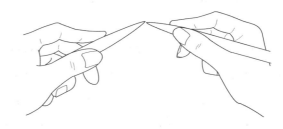

Like a knife
Pick up the needles, one in each hand, as if you were holding a knife and fork—that is to say, with your hands lightly over the top of each needle. As you knit, you will tuck the blunt end of the right-hand needle under your arm, let go with your hand and use your hand to manipulate the yarn, returning your hand to the needle to move the stitches along.

Like a pen
Now try changing the right hand so you are holding the needle as you would hold a pen, with your thumb and forefinger lightly gripping the needle close to its pointed tip and the shaft resting in the crook of your thumb. As you knit, you will not need to let go of the needle but simply slide your right hand forward to manipulate the yarn.

Holding yarn

As you knit, you will be working stitches off the left needle and onto the right needle, and the yarn you are working with needs to be tensioned and manipulated to produce an even fabric. To hold and tension the yarn you can use either your right or left hand. Try both methods to discover which works best for you.

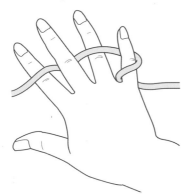

Yarn in right hand
With the ball of yarn on the right, catch the yarn around your little finger then lace it over the third finger, under the middle finger, and over the first finger of your right hand.

Yarn in left hand
With the ball of yarn on your left, catch the yarn around your little finger then take it over the third and middle fingers. Most left-handed knitters will also find that, even if they reverse the direction of knitting (working stitches off the right needle onto the left needle), using the left hand to manipulate the yarn will be easier to manage. To knit and purl in the Continental style (see pages 117 and 118), hold the yarn in your left hand.

Making a slip knot

You will need to make a slip knot to form your first cast-on stitch.

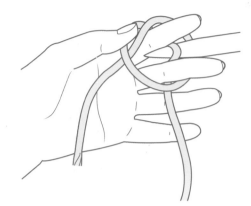

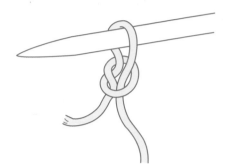

1 With the ball of yarn on your right, lay the end of the yarn on the palm of your left hand and hold it in place with your left thumb. With your right hand, take the yarn round your top two fingers to form a loop. Take the knitting needle through the back of the loop from right to left and use it to pick up the strand nearest to the yarn ball, as shown in the diagram. Pull the strand through to form a loop at the front.

2 Slip the yarn off your fingers leaving the loop on the needle. Gently pull on both yarn ends to tighten the knot. Then pull on the yarn leading to the ball of yarn to tighten the knot on the needle.

Casting on (cable method)

There are a few methods of casting on but the one used for the projects in this book is the cable method, which uses two needles.

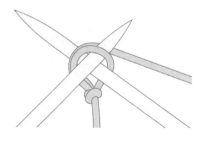

1 Make a slip knot as shown above. Put the needle with the slip knot into your left hand. Insert the point of your other needle into the front of the slip knot and under the left needle. Wind the yarn from the ball of yarn around the tip of the right needle.

2 Using the tip of your needle, draw the yarn through the slip knot to form a loop. This loop is your new stitch. Slip the loop from the right needle onto the left needle.

3 To make the next stitch, insert the tip of your right needle between the two stitches. Wind the yarn over the right needle, from left to right, then draw the yarn through to form a loop. Transfer this loop to your left needle. Repeat until you have cast on the right number of stitches for your project.

Basic stitches

Most people in the English-speaking world knit using a method called English (or American) knitting. However, in parts of Europe, people prefer a method known as Continental knitting. If you are new to knitting, try both techniques to see which works better for you.

Making a knit stitch

1 Hold the needle with the cast-on stitches in your left hand, and then insert the point of the right needle into the front of the first stitch from left to right. Wind the yarn around the point of the right needle, from left to right.

2 With the tip of your right needle, pull the yarn through the stitch to form a loop. This loop is your new stitch.

3 Slip the original stitch off the left needle by gently pulling your right needle to the right. Repeat these steps till you have knitted all the stitches on your left needle. To work the next row, transfer the needle with all the stitches into your left hand.

Making a knit stitch Continental style

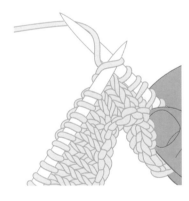 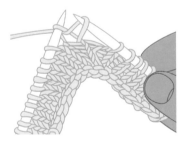 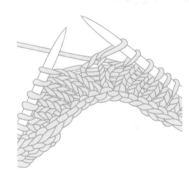

1 Hold the needle with the stitches to be knitted in your left hand, and then insert the tip of the right needle into the front of the first stitch from left to right. Holding the yarn fairly taut with your left hand at the back of your work, use the tip of your right needle to pick up a loop of yarn.

2 With the tip of your right needle, bring the yarn through the original stitch to form a loop. This loop is your new stitch.

3 Slip the original stitch off the left needle by gently pulling your right needle to the right. Repeat these steps till you have knitted all the stitches on your left needle. To work the next row, transfer the needle with all the stitches into your left hand.

Making a purl stitch

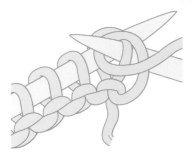

1 Hold the needle with the stitches in your left hand, and then insert the point of the right needle into the front of the first stitch from right to left. Wind the yarn around the point of the right needle, from right to left.

2 With the tip of the right needle, pull the yarn through the stitch to form a loop. This loop is your new stitch.

3 Slip the original stitch off the left needle by gently pulling your right needle to the right. Repeat these steps till you have purled all the stitches on your left needle. To work the next row, transfer the needle with all the stitches into your left hand.

Making a purl stitch Continental style

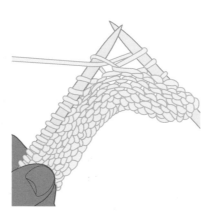

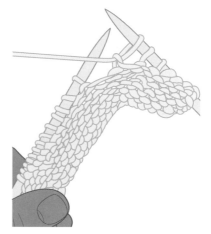

1 Hold the needle with the stitches to be knitted in your left hand, and then insert the tip of the right needle into the front of the first stitch from right to left. Holding the yarn fairly taut at the front of your work, use the tip of your right needle to pick up a loop of yarn.

2 With the tip of your right needle, bring the yarn through the original stitch to form a loop.

3 Slip the original stitch off the left needle by gently pulling your right needle to the right. Repeat these steps till you have purled all the stitches on your left needle. To work the next row, transfer the needle with all the stitches into your left hand.

Binding (casting) off

You need to bind (cast) off your stitches to complete the projects and stop the knitting unraveling.

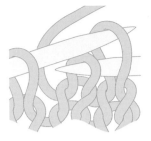

1 First knit two stitches in the normal way. With the point of your left needle, pick up the first stitch you have just knitted and lift it over the second stitch. Knit another stitch so that there are two stitches on your needle again. Repeat the process of lifting the first stitch over the second stitch. Continue this process until there is just one stitch remaining on the right needle.

2 Break the yarn, leaving a tail of yarn long enough to stitch your work together. Pull the tail all the way through the last stitch. Slip the stitch off the needle and pull it fairly tightly to make sure it is secure.

Knitted fabrics

Only simple combinations of knit and purl stitches are used for most of the projects in this book.

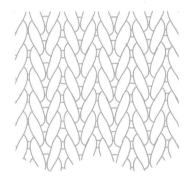

Stockinette (stocking) stitch

To make this stitch, work alternate rows of knit and purl stitches. The front of the fabric is the side facing you as you work the knit rows. This stitch is used for the main part of most of the projects.

Garter stitch

To make this stitch, you simply knit every row. This stitch is often used for borders and to add texture.

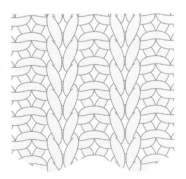

Rib

To make this stitch, you knit 1 stitch then purl 1 stitch across a row. On the next row, you knit the purl stitches and purl the knit stitches. Rib is used on the cuffs of mitts and socks in this book.

Increasing

There are two methods of increasing used in this book.

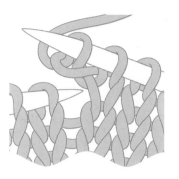

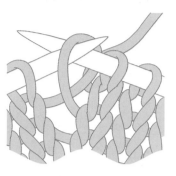

Increase (inc)

Start knitting your stitch in the normal way but instead of slipping the "old" stitch off the needle, knit into the back of it and then slip the "old" stitch off the needle in the normal way. The same principle is used to increase on a purl row, except that you purl the stitches instead of knitting them.

Make one (m1)

Pick up the horizontal strand between two stitches on your left-hand needle. Knit into the back of the loop and transfer the stitch to the right-hand needle in the normal way. (It is important to knit into the back of the loop so that the yarn is twisted and does not form a hole in your work.)

Decreasing

There are three different ways of decreasing used in this book.

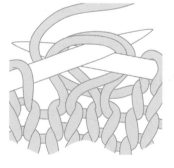

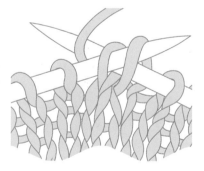

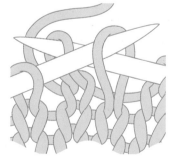

Knit two together (k2tog)

This is the simplest way of decreasing. Simply insert your needle through two stitches instead of the normal one when you begin your stitch and then knit them in the normal way. The same principle is used to decrease on a purl row, except that you purl the stitches together instead of knitting them.

Slip, slip, knit (ssk)

Slip one stitch knitwise, and then the next stitch knitwise onto your right-hand needle, without knitting them. Then insert the left-hand needle from left to right through the front loops of both the slipped stitches and knit them as normal.

Slip one, knit one, pass the slipped stitch over (skpo)

Slip the first stitch knitwise from the left to the right needle without knitting it. Knit the next stitch. Then lift the slipped stitch over the knitted stitch and drop it off the needle.

Knitting in different colors

If you are knitting in stripes, you can simply join in the second color at the end of a row.
If the stripes are narrow, you do not need to break and rejoin your yarn between stripes.

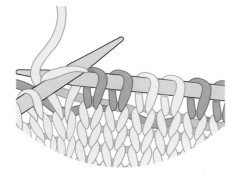 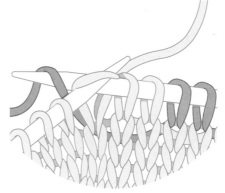

Stranding

If you are knitting just a few stitches in a different color, you can simply leave the color
you are not using on the wrong side of the work and pick it up again when you need to.

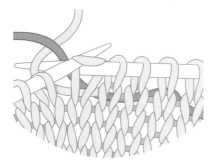

Weaving

If you are knitting more than a few stitches in a different color, but only for a
few rows, you can weave the yarns into the back of the stitches as you work.
On a knit row, insert your right-hand needle into the next stitch and lay the
yarn you want to weave in over the needle. Knit the stitch, taking it under the
yarn you are weaving in, making sure to pull through only the main yarn.
Repeat this every few stitches until you need to use the second yarn again.
On a purl row, use the same method to work in the yarn.

Intarsia color change

If you are knitting blocks of different colors within a project, which you will need to do for some
projects in this book, you will need to use a technique called intarsia. This involves using separate
balls of yarn for each area and twisting the yarns together where they join to avoid creating a gap.

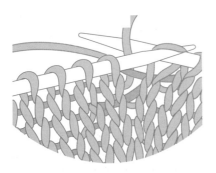 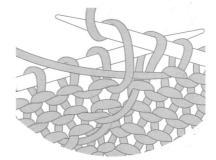

On the right side

When you want to change colors and the color change is
vertical or sloping to the right, take the first color over the
second color. Then pick up the second color, so the strands of
yarn cross each other.

On the wrong side

This is worked in almost the same way as on the right side.
When you want to change colors and the color change is
vertical or sloping to the left, take the first color over the
second color. Then pick up the second color, so the strands of
yarn cross each other.

Picking up stitches

For some projects, you will need to pick up stitches along either a horizontal edge (the cast-on or bound-/cast-off edge of your knitting), or a vertical edge (the edges of your rows of knitting).

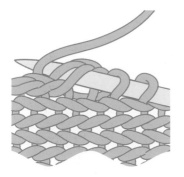

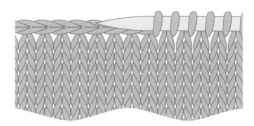

Along a vertical edge

With the right side of the knitting facing you, insert a knitting needle from the front to back between the first and second stitches of the first row. Wind the yarn around the needle and pull through a loop to form the new stitch. Normally you have more gaps between rows than stitches you need to pick up and knit. To make sure your picking up is even, you will have to miss a gap every few rows.

Along a horizontal edge

This is worked in the same way as picking up stitches along a vertical edge, except that you will work through the cast-on stitches rather than the gaps between rows. You will normally have the same number of stitches to pick up and knit as there are existing stitches.

Knitting in the round

Knitting in the round, or circular knitting as it is also known, is a way of producing a tube of knitting with no seam.

You can knit in the round on circular needles, which consist of a flexible plastic wire with a short pointed knitting needle at each end. Or you can use a set of four or five double-pointed needles (DPNs). For small projects like socks, most people use DPNs because standard circular needles are too long. However you can now buy shorter circular needles, specially designed for smaller projects, in specialist shops and online stores.

When you knit on DPNs, you divide your stitches evenly between three or four needles, and use the fourth or fifth needle to knit with. When you knit in the round, you knit each row (rather than work alternating rows of knit and purl stitches) to form stockinette (stocking) stitch.

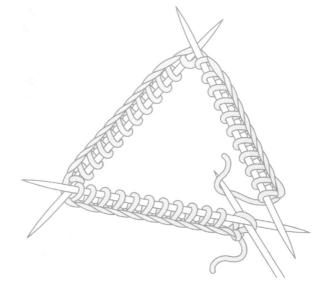

Crochet edging

A crochet edging gives a neat decorative finish to a piece of knitting.

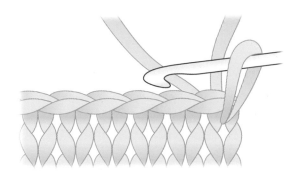

1 Insert the crochet hook in the first space between stitches. Wind the yarn round the hook and pull a loop of yarn through.

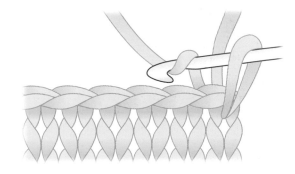

2 Wind the yarn round the hook again and then pull the loop through to make a single chain.

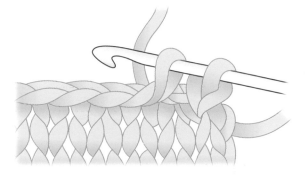

3 Insert the hook through the next stitch, wind the yarn round the hook, and pull through a second loop of yarn.

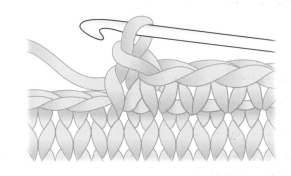

4 Wind the yarn round the hook and pull a loop of yarn through both loops on the hook. Repeat steps 3 and 4, inserting the hook into the spaces between stitches in an even pattern. For crochet edging along a vertical edge, insert your hook into the spaces between the edges of the rows rather than the spaces between stitches.

Embroidery stitches

The animals' features are embroidered using knitting yarn. When embroidering on knitting, take the embroidery needle in and out of the work between the strands that make up the yarn rather than between the knitted stitches themselves; this will help make your embroidery look more even.

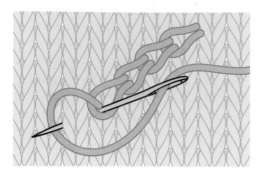

Chain stitch

Bring the yarn out at the starting point on the front of the work. Take your needle back into your knitting just next to the starting point, leaving a loop of yarn. Bring your needle out of the work again, a stitch length further on and catch in the loop. Pull the thread up firmly, but not so tight that it pulls the knitting. Continue in this way till the line, coil, or circle is complete.

Straight stitch

To make this stitch, simply take the yarn out at the starting point and back down into the work where you want the stitch to end.

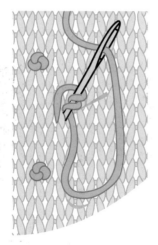

French knots

Bring the yarn out at the starting point, where you want the French knot to sit. Wind the yarn around your needle the required number of times, then take it back into the work, just to the side of the starting point. Then bring your needle out at the point for the next French knot or, if you are working the last or a single knot, to the back of your work. Continue pulling your needle through the work and slide the knot off the needle and onto the knitting.

Lazy daisy stitch

These are individual chain stitches. Bring the yarn out at the starting point on the front of the work. Take your needle back into your knitting just next to the starting point, leaving a loop of yarn. Bring your needle out of the work again, a stitch length further on, and catch in the loop. Make a small straight stitch over the end of the loop to hold it in place and bring the needle out at the point for the next lazy daisy stitch.

Mattress stitch

There are two versions of this stitch—one used to join two vertical edges and the other used to join two horizontal edges.

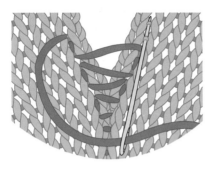

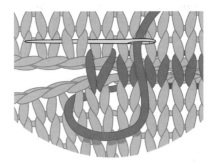

Vertical edges

Place the two edges side by side with the right side facing you. Take a yarn sewing needle under the running thread between the first two stitches of one side, then under the corresponding running thread of the other side. Pull your yarn up fairly firmly every few stitches.

Horizontal edges

Place the two edges side by side with the right side facing you. Take a yarn sewing needle under the two "legs" of the last row of stitches on the first piece of knitting. Then take your needle under the two "legs" of the corresponding stitch on the second piece of knitting. Pull your yarn up fairly firmly every few stitches.

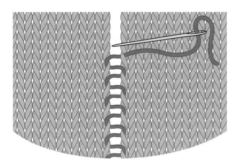

Flat stitch

Unlike mattress stitch, this stitch creates a join that is completely flat.

Lay the two edges to be joined side by side with the right side facing you. Using a yarn sewing needle, pick up the very outermost strand of knitting from one side and then the other, working your way along the seam and pulling your yarn up firmly every few stitches.

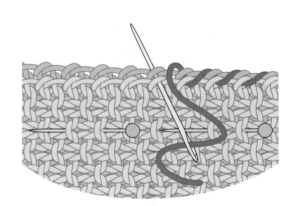

Oversewing

This stitch is used to seam small pieces of work. It is normally worked with the right sides of the work together. Take the yarn from the front of the work, over the edge of the seam, and out through the front again a short distance further on.

Sewing in ends

The easiest way to finish yarn ends is to run a few small stitches forward then backward through your work, ideally in a seam. It is a good idea to use a yarn sewing needle to do this and take the tail between the strands that make up your yarn, as this will help make sure the tail stays in place.

Abbreviations

beg	begin(ning)
C3R	cable 3 right: slip next 2 stitches onto cable needle and hold at back of work, knit next stitch from left-hand needle then knit stitches from cable needle.
C3L	cable 3 left: slip next stitch onto cable needle and hold at front of work, knit next 2 stitches from left-hand needle then knit stitches from cable needle.
cm	centimeter(s)
cont	continue
g	gram(s)
in	inch(es)
inc	increase, by working into front and back of next stitch: see page 120
k	knit
k2tog	knit two stitches together, to decrease: see page 120
kwise	knitwise
m1	make one stitch, by knitting into the strand between two stitches, to increase: see page 120
m	meter(s)
mm	millimeter
oz	ounces
p	purl
p2tog	purl two stitches together, to decrease: see *Knit two together*, page 120
psso	pass slipped stitch over, pass a slipped stitch over another stitch
p2sso	pass two slipped stitches over, pass two slipped stitches over another stitch

pwise	purlwise
rem	remain(ing)
rep	repeat
RS	right side
skpo	slip one stitch, knit one stitch, pass slipped stitch over knitted one, to decrease: see page 120
sl1(2)	slip one (two) stitch(es), from the left-hand needle to the right-hand needle without knitting it (them)
ssk	slip one stitch, slip one stitch, knit slipped stitches together, to decrease: see page 120
st(s)	stitch(es)
st st	stockinette (stocking) stitch
tbl	through the back loop, knit or purl though the back of the stitch
WS	wrong side
WT	with yarn at the back, slip the next stitch purlwise from the left-hand to the right-hand needle. Bring the yarn forward between the needles. Slip the stitch from the right-hand needle back to the left-hand needle. Take the yarn back between the needles. Turn the work.
yb	yarn back, between the tips of the needles
yd	yard(s)
yf	yarn forward, between the tips of the needles
yo	yarnover, wrap yarn around needle between stitches, to increase and to make an eyelet
[ ]	work instructions within square brackets as directed
*****	work instructions after/between asterisk(s) as directed

Author's acknowledgments

My thanks to Cindy Richards, Penny Craig, Fahema Khanam, and everyone at CICO Books for their ideas and hard work. Thanks also to Kate Haxell, my editor, Marilyn Wilson, the pattern checker, Terry Benson, the photographer, and Rob Merrett, the stylist. I would also like to thank my sister Louise Turner for help with the knitting and my husband Roger Dromard and our son Louis for not minding when the house looks like a knitting workshop. Lastly, thanks to my parents Paddy and David Goble for always being interested in what I'm doing.

Suppliers

This is a list of some of the major suppliers of the yarns used in this book. For reasons of space, we cannot cover all stockists so please explore the local knitting shops and online stores in your own country. Please remember that from time to time companies will change the brands they supply or stock and will not always offer the full range. If you cannot find a particular yarn locally, there will usually be an excellent alternative and your local yarn store is the best place to ask about this.

USA

Knitting Fever Inc.
Trade distributor
www.knittingfever.com
Facility on website to find your nearest knitting store (no direct sales)
Debbie Bliss, Katia, Sirdar, Sublime

JO-ANN FABRIC AND CRAFT STORES
Retail stores and online
www.joann.com
Store locator on website
Lion Brand, Patons

LION BRAND YARNS
Online store for Lion Brand yarns
Tel: +800 258 YARN (9276)
www.lionbrand.com
Stockist locator on website (USA, Mexico & Canada)

Canada

DIAMOND YARN
Trade distributor
Tel: +1 416 736 6111
www.diamondyarn.com
Stockist locator on website (no direct sales)
Debbie Bliss, Hayfield, Katia, Sirdar, Sublime

DGB CANADA
Trade distributor
Tel: +1 888 749 7559
www.dgbcanada.com
Stockist locator on website (no direct sales)
Phildar

UK

DERAMORES
Online store only
Tel: 0800 488 0708
www.deramores.com
Bergere de France, Erika Knight, Hayfield, Katia, King Cole, Lion Brand, Patons, Phildar, Rowan, Sublime, UK Alpaca

JOHN LEWIS
Retail stores and online
Tel: 03456 049049
www.johnlewis.com
Telephone numbers of stores on website
Debbie Bliss, Erika Knight, Patons, Rowan, Sirdar, Sublime, Wendy

LAUGHING HENS
Online store only
Tel: +44 (0) 1829 740903
www.laughinghens.com
Bergere de France, Debbie Bliss, King Cole, Patons, Rowan, Sublime, Wendy

MAVIS CRAFTS
Retail store and online
Tel: +44 (0) 208 950 5445
www.mavis-crafts.com
Hayfield, Katia, Sirdar, Sublime, Wendy

Australia

Black Sheep Wool 'n' Wares
Retail store and online
Tel: +61 (0)2 6779 1196
www.blacksheepwool.com.au
Debbie Bliss, King Cole, Katia, Patons, Sirdar, Sublime, Wendy

SUN SPUN
Retail store only (Canterbury, Victoria)
Tel: +61 (0)3 9830 1609
Debbie Bliss, Rowan, Sublime

TEXYARNS INTERNATIONAL PTY LTD
Trade distributor
Tel: +61 (0)3 9427 9009
www.texyarns.com
Stockist locator on website (no direct sales)
Katia

Finding a yarn stockist in your country

The following websites will help you find stockists for these yarn brands in your country. Please note that not all brands or types of yarn will be available in all countries.

BERGERE DE FRANCE
www.bergeredefrance.com

KATIA YARNS
Tel: +34 93 828 38 19
www.katia.com

ROWAN YARNS
Tel: +44 (0) 1484 681881
www.knitrowan.com

SIRDAR (INC. HAYFIELD & SUBLIME)
Tel: +44 (0) 1924 231682
www.sirdar.co.uk

index